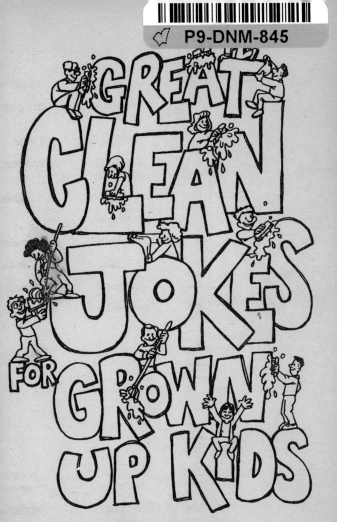

# GREAT CLEAN JOKES FOR GROWN UP KIDS

Compiled and Edited by
Dan Harmon

BARBOUR
PUBLISHING, INC.
Uhrichsville, Ohio

© MCMXCVI by Barbour Publishing, Inc.

ISBN 1-55748-903-3

All rights reserved. No part of this publication may be reproduced or transmitted in any form or by any means without written permission of the publisher.

Published by  Barbour Publishing, Inc.
P.O. Box 719
Uhrichsville, Ohio 44683
http://www.barbourbooks.com

Member of the
Evangelical Christian
Publishers Association

Printed in the United States of America.

# Introduction

Martin Luther once threw up his hands and proclaimed, "The devil should not be allowed to keep all the best tunes for himself." Shortly thereafter, the "Lutheran Lyricist" proceeded to pen "A Mighty Fortress Is Our God," one of the most popular hymns of all time, and the Christmas hymn "From Heaven Above to Earth I Come."

Luther's challenge has become my life's mission. Put another way, the devil should not be allowed to dictate what passes for good music. . .or good jokes. Why not then reclaim *humor* for the Lord, truly the Author of All Things Humorous?

*Great Clean Jokes for Grown-Up Kids* is my humble attempt to make you laugh without holding any fellow human in contempt. It's okay to laugh at lawyers in general—but only as long as you're willing to cross-examine their contentious clients. And yes, it's okay to chortle at medical professionals, but only as long as you're willing to put under a high-powered microscope their pesky patients.

Today's brand of popular humor is based on sarcasm and vulgarity. Take away those unnecessary and ungodly elements and the joy of the human situation—which our Lord Himself surely relishes with holy delight (and paternal love)—still remains.

I am most grateful to my human sounding boards, sources, and assistants, including Courtney Harmon; Jan and Christi Kotowski; Connie Robinette; Mr. and Mrs. Francis Cone; Jeff, Cari and Mike Cone; Greg Arnell; Jack Kreismer; and especially Sherie, Jessica, and Alison Manner.

Thanks be to God, who has blessed us, more than we know, with the ability to laugh at ourselves.

# ANIMALS

A couple sat in a movie theater with their pet bulldog. During the action scenes, the dog's ears perked up and he barked excitedly. During the sad scenes, his eyes glazed with moisture.

The woman seated next to them was amazed. "That," she remarked as they all left the theater, "is astonishing. I've never seen an animal react to a movie that way."

"It is baffling," the husband replied, shaking his head.

"Yes," agreed the wife. "Boxie positively hated the book."

• • • •

A small boy ran to his grandfather, babbling with excitement. "Guess what we saw at the circus! There was a man dressed in gold and black riding a big white horse, and he rode around the ring standing on one foot on the horse's back, and then he grabbed the horse's mane and swung down underneath the neck, and came up on the other side, and ended up riding backward!"

The old man puffed slowly on his pipe. "Actually," he mused, "I did that one time when I was about 16 years old."

"You did? Wow! How'd you stop the horse?"

"I didn't. I just fell off."

• • • •

"I heard you bought a pet zebra. What's its name?"
"Spot."

Mrs. James answered the front doorbell one day to find her dear old friend Mrs. Avery standing outside with a huge, mangy, panting dog. Delighted by the unexpected visit, Mrs. James bade her friend inside. The dog bounded ahead of them, knocked over a valuable vase while dashing for the cat, used the lush carpet as a toilet, then jumped onto an antique sofa and proceeded to take a nap.

He was still napping an hour later when Mrs. Avery rose to leave. Mrs. James showed her to the door and waited for her to call the dog. But her friend paid no attention whatsoever to the animal.

"Aren't you going to take your animal with you?" Mrs. James asked, a hint of impatience in her voice.

"Oh, that awful beast is not my pet. I thought he was yours."

• • • •

A woman accidentally ran over her neighbor's cat while driving down the street. She stopped, very upset, and ran to the door to apologize.

"I'd like to replace it," she told the neighbor.

"Really? You know how to catch mice?"

• • • •

Mary had a little lamb,
A little cake, a little Spam,
A banana split, three onion rings,
Some tofu and threw up.

• • • •

How did scientists determine that carrots
are good for vision?
Out of a test group of 30 rabbits,
none required glasses.

A man brought his dog to a veterinarian's office. The animal was quite stiff and seemed, to all appearances, dead. But the man wanted to make sure.

So the vet examined the corpse thoroughly and pronounced with certainty that the dog had indeed passed away. The man, very upset, asked, "Is there nothing at all you can do? I have to be absolutely certain little Morty is gone before I can begin to deal with it and find peace."

The vet thought a moment, then whispered to an assistant, who went into another room and returned momentarily with a live cat. The cat was placed on the table beside the dog and sniffed the corpse from one end to the other. Then it hopped down from the table and walked back into the other room.

"No question whatsoever," the veterinarian said. "Morty is dead."

The vet then wrote out a bill for $200.

"I don't understand," the man said in dismay. "You're charging me $200 to verify the death of my dog?"

"Not exactly," the vet explained. "My examination was $50. The other $150 is for the cat scan."

• • • •

A visitor at a zoo commented to one of the animal tenders, "I wonder what that tiger would say if it could talk."

"Probably one of the first things it would tell you is, 'I'm a mountain lion.' "

• • • •

"How are your little girls?" asked Mrs. McKenzie.

"Lovely," said Mrs. Baines. "Just started school, and they're excited."

"And how are all their little animals?"

"Average. One of the goldfish died and the other one won't."

A cross between a whale and a duck:
Moby Duckling.

• • • •

It's said the hippopotamus never forgets things. But what, exactly, would a hippopotamus need to remember?

• • • •

A family was at the zoo watching an elephant snarf up peanuts with its trunk.

"Daddy," the small daughter asked, "is that long thing in front a vacuum cleaner?"

# BIRDS

Two small birds in a big city agreed to meet at a certain elm tree in the park for lunch. One arrived at the designated tree a bit early and waited. . .and waited, and waited, and waited. Figuring the other had forgotten their appointment, this bird was about to fly away when it noticed in the distance, hobbling across the grass, a tiny creature. As it slowly approached, the newcomer was seen to be the tardy little bird. Its feathers were horribly ruffled and the pitiable bird was in a daze.

"What has happened to you?" asked the friend. "Did you encounter an airplane?"

"No," whispered the disheveled one. "I arrived at the other end of the park awhile ago and noticed a lot of people gathered in a clearing. I flew down to see what was going on, and the next thing I knew, I was playing badminton."

A man went to a pet shop and asked for a bird that could sing. The proprietor brought out a gorgeous tropical bird, looked the bird in the eye, puckered his lips and started to whistle. The bird took up the very note and finished the tune with him.

"That's mighty fine," the customer said, "but I'd never pay money for that bird. His right leg's crippled."

"I thought you wanted me to sing!" cried the bird. "I gotta dance, too?"

• • • •

A couple at a pet auction had to bid unexpectedly high to win the bird they'd been eyeing—a cute, green Quaker parrot.

"I sure hope this bird can talk," the husband told the official as they paid for the bird.

"Of course. It's been talking all night," the official said.

"Really? We didn't notice much bird noise during the auction."

And the bird cracked, "Who do you think was bidding against you?"

• • • •

The family parrot had been a huge disappointment, not saying a word the first six months they owned it. Suddenly, as the child placed the bird's food container inside its cage one day, the parrot squawked, "It's moldy! It's moldy!"

The child was ecstatic. "Did you hear that, Dad?! Polly said her first words!"

The family gathered round the cage. "Very strange," said the mother. "Wonder why Polly hasn't said anything before."

The parrot piped up, "Food's been fine 'til today."

# BOASTING

A western rancher and an eastern farmer were bragging on the comparative sizes of their domains. Claimed the rancher, "I can get in my truck at dawn, start at the south edge of my range, drive north all day long, and at sunset I'll still be on my own spread."

"Yeah," muttered the farmer, "we used to have an old truck like that."

• • • •

"I'm rather proud of my self-control," remarked Paul. "I've stopped smoking and stuck to it now for two weeks."

"That's simply a matter of commitment," responded his father. "Real self-control is stopping the habit and refraining from telling anyone."

• • • •

A foreign tourist riding through New York City for the first time gazed upward at a skyscraper. "What do you call that building?" he asked the cabby.

"The World Trade Center."

"Hmm. I have heard of it, and I am surprised at how small it really is. In my country, we can complete such a structure in approximately 10 days. And what is the one ahead of us on the left?"

"I dunno. It wasn't there yesterday."

# CHILDREN

Mom and Dad were getting started with Saturday chores when their child came out into the yard. "Why don't you go across the street and ask how old Mrs. Wells is this morning?" Dad suggested.

The child dutifully crossed the street, greeted their neighbor three doors down and put the question: "Dad wants to know how old you are this morning."

Back home, the child reported to his parents, "Mrs. Wells said to tell you to mind your own business."

• • • •

"How's your husband doing with the baby?" a woman asked her friend.

"He's learning. Last night he figured out that you don't wake little Sherie up in order to see her smile."

• • • •

It had been a very long day, and the mother had had it up to the eyebrows with problems and commotion. "If you don't turn down that rap CD," she shrieked to her teen-age son, "I'll go absolutely bananas!"

"It may be too late," her son said sheepishly. "I turned it off about 15 minutes ago."

• • • •

"I hear you have your brother's children spending the week with you," Darlene said to her friend Marla. "Counting your two, that makes five kids in one house. Wow! How are you feeling?"

"Outnumbered."

Two parents were sorting out the details of a fight between their children. After a few moments of chaos as both youths shouted simultaneous versions of what had occurred, the parents called for quiet and asked them to report in turn.

"It all started," explained Dennis, trying to sound calm, "when Jeremy hit me back."

• • • •

It's said that Albert Einstein was visited regularly in the afternoons by the 8-year-old daughter of a neighboring family. The mother apologized, but Einstein assured her it was a mutually beneficial friendship: He liked the jelly-beans the girl brought him, and the youngster liked the way Einstein helped her with arithmetic.

• • • •

"Mommy, Randall just broke the bedroom window!"

"Oh, no! How did that happen?"

"I threw a shoe at him, and he ducked."

• • • •

A girl ran downstairs into the living room just as her parents were commenting on who her little brother looked like.

"I think he has your eyes," Mother was saying.

"And your nose," Father was adding.

"And now he's got Grandma's teeth!" the daughter interrupted.

"Grandpa, what do you do all day long?" asked little Jimmy, coming home from school.

"Get a little older, son."

• • • •

A little boy had been locked in his room for misbehaving. Mischievous tike that he was, he picked the lock and ran into the hallway shouting, "I'm free! I'm free!"

His sister was playing in the hallway. "That's nothing," she said. "I'm four."

• • • •

A couple returned home from a party about 2 a.m. and noticed their neighbor pacing back and forth on his darkened front porch.

"Can we help you?" they called across the yard.

"No," he said huffily. "I forgot my keys and I've been waiting for my teen-age daughter to come home and unlock the door."

• • • •

A woman was admiring her friend's newborn son. "He certainly favors his father," she said.

"You're right about that. Sleeps all the time, doesn't say anything and doesn't have any hair."

• • • •

A little boy went to the pet shop to buy a new food dish for his dog.

"Would you like to have your dog's name on the bowl?" the clerk asked.

"No, thanks. She can't read."

"How much money do you think I'm worth, Dad?"

The father regarded his teen-age son thoughtfully. "To your mother and me, I would say you're priceless."

"Do you think I'm worth a thousand dollars?"

"Certainly."

"A million?"

"Even more than a million, to us."

"Would you mind giving me about twenty of it, then?"

• • • •

What's the best way to keep children from
overhearing what you're saying?
Say it to them.

• • • •

A friendly neighbor mosied over to his lawn fence and beckoned the two boys playing on the other side. When they approached, he held up a baseball.

"Does this belong to either of you?"

"Did it damage anything on your side of the fence?" asked one boy timidly.

"Yes, I'm afraid it broke my kitchen window."

"It's not ours," said the second boy.

• • • •

A little boy, unhappy at not getting his way, screwed his face into a terrible pout. His grandfather, hoping to demonstrate how silly the expression looked, screwed up his own face and confronted the child eye to eye. The boy's angry countenance turned to bewilderment. "What's bothering *you?*" he asked.

Little Jerome dashed in from school very excited. "Mommy!" he shouted. "I've learned to count!"

"Wonderful! Let me hear you."

"One, two, three, four, five."

The mother nodded and raised her eyebrows expectantly. "That's right. Go on. . . ."

Jerome frowned. "You mean there's more?"

• • • •

"I don't like cheese with holes in it," grumbled the unhappy child.

"All right, dear," obliged the mother. "You can leave the holes. Just eat the cheese."

• • • •

Jerry shuffled timidly into the living room to tell his father, "You know how you've been telling me not to play with your fly rod in the backyard because you're worried I'll break it?"

"Yes. And. . . ?"

"Well, there's no need to worry anymore."

• • • •

"Cleanliness may be next to godliness for most people," a woman told a friend, "but for my little Georgie, it's next to impossible."

• • • •

"Grandpa, have you ever been wrong?"asked little Beverly.

"Oh, one time I thought I was, but I was obviously mistaken."

Max thought it was cool being the son of a noted computer programmer until he came home from school one day, sacked out in front of the TV set like always, and saw this streamer cross the screen: WE INTERRUPT THIS PROGRAM BECAUSE WE HAVE SERIOUS REASON TO BELIEVE YOU HAVEN'T DONE YOUR HOMEWORK.

• • • •

"You're being very sarcastic today, Jenny. Where did you learn to talk like that?"

"Shakespeare."

"Well I think you should stop playing with him."

• • • •

Mrs. Ormand: "I'm afraid our child Emily has a bit of an ego problem."

Mrs. Black: "How do you mean?"

Mrs. Ormand: "We celebrated her birthday last week. We gave her the gifts and told her 'Happy Birthday!' and she told us, 'Congratulations!' "

• • • •

The new mom was a frazzled basket case. "The baby cries all the time," she complained to friends.

"Maybe he needs to have his diaper changed more often," volunteered a sympathetic veteran.

"Change his diaper? Oh, no, I don't have to do that yet."

"What? You don't change his diaper?!"

"Of course not," replied the mother. "Says on the box it's good for up to 15 pounds."

Brittany came to her mother and asked, "Mommy, do you know what you look like?"

"Why, yes. I think I do."

"That's good, because Brenda and I just broke your bedroom mirror."

. . . .

"Daryl, go wash your hands for dinner," his mother commanded.

"But Mom, only one hand is dirty."

"Okay. If you think you can wash just that one, you're welcome to try."

. . . .

Tommy came into the kitchen and asked for an apple, which his mother immediately provided. A few minutes later he was back for a second—then a third.

"What is this?" his mother scolded. "You're eating every apple we have in the house. They don't grow on trees, you know."

. . . .

Mom: "That's a bad word! Where did you learn to talk like that?"

Son: "From Santa Claus."

Mom: "Santa Claus? What do you mean?"

Son: "That's what he said when he knocked over the Christmas tree."

# THE COLLEGE SCENE

A philosophy instructor was going over a test paper with a failing student. The instructor frowned. "It's a poor conclusion of this example of logic," he said.

The student shrugged. "I guess I wasn't thinking of it as a conclusion. That's just the place where I got tired of thinking about it."

• • • •

A news editing professor grading the results of a proofreading test was devastated to notice this sentence in his own instructions: "Read slowly and carefully to sure nothing missing."

• • • •

An ethics professor called on a student to resolve a hypothetical issue in class. The student declined. "I have no solution—but I really admire the problem."

• • • •

A bright farm boy announced to his weathered old dad, "I've decided to go to medical school and study anesthesiology."

"I wouldn't, if I were you, boy," the father said. "By the time you graduate, they'll have a cure for it."

• • • •

A biology professor was giving a popular science lecture at a small-town library. His subject was whales. "Even a young whale consumes hundreds of pounds of plankton every day," he remarked.

An elderly man in the rear of the room, hard of hearing, leaned toward the lady sitting next to him. "Whose boy did he say does that?"

Farmer Zeke: "Well, I reckon my boy's home from college."

Farmer Bill: "Whaddya mean, you 'reckon?' Don't you know?"

Farmer Zeke: "All we know is we haven't heard from him in the last three days, and the car's gone."

. . . .

An astronomy student approached his professor at the end of class and said, "I'm beginning to understand how we calculate the distances to stars light years away. But how did we ever find out their names?"

. . . .

An American scholar was mortified to be seated next to a foreign scholar at a faculty luncheon. He wanted to make the guest feel warmly welcomed, but he had no idea how to break the ice. The visitor, for his part, was ill at ease and silent. The professor assumed this indicated a problem understanding the English language.

"You. . .er. . .likee steakee?" the American ventured.

The foreigner looked puzzled, then seemed to understand. "Ummm," he said, nodding. And that was as far as the conversation went during dinner.

After the meal, to the American's surprise, the student was invited to the podium to make a few remarks. The American was completely shocked when the visitor, in perfect English, warmed up the audience with a few jokes, then expressed a graceful thank-you for the hospitality he'd received.

Returning to his seat, the guest asked the American, "Likee speechee?"

A journalism professor admonished her news writing class: "Never employ an obscure, 50-cent word if a Lilliputian alternate will serve just as well."

• • • •

Several professors were taking their leisure in the faculty lounge when the conversation turned to dreams. They in turn recounted some of their memorable recent dreams and shared their thoughts as to the origins.

Then the doyen of the college shared his experience. "I dreamed last week I was lecturing a philosophy class. Then I woke up and discovered I was lecturing a philosophy class."

# COMPUTERS

The first passenger spaceship to the moon was underway, and as the excited passengers adapted to the weightless comfort of their seats, a kind, reassuring voice came over the intercom.

"Welcome aboard the Lunar Liner, ladies and gentlemen. We hope you are finding everything to your liking. We want to remind you the Liner is a multibillion-dollar, state-of-the-art vehicle. It has undergone years of thorough testing and refinement. Nothing possibly can go wrong with the equipment. And as you probably have been informed already, the vessel is crewed entirely by computers, eliminating any chance for human error human error human error human. . ."

A computer salesman was trying to talk a customer into buying a high-speed, high-priced, brand new, barely tested machine.

"But the other one has all I really need," she objected. "I don't care if the technology is six months old. I'm only going to use it for word processing. What's wrong with it?"

"Speed," said the clerk, shaking his head, "The new machine reboots much, much faster."

A man passing by in the aisle whispered, "And much more often."

• • • •

Another technology lecturer was asked when he thought America might arrive at the era of the fabled "paperless office," when all documents and correspondence are created, communicated, and stored totally by computer. "We'll have the paperless office," he intoned, "approximately the same year we have the paperless toilet."

• • • •

The clerk had had it up to the hair follicles with the office computer, which seemed to crash every 10 minutes. Hours of futile phone calls to tech support and long waits on permahold yielded no solutions. Finally, she managed to contact one of the programmers of the software she was using. She gave the programmer a detailed description of the problems, concluding, "And that manual of yours is no help at all. We can't understand a word it says."

The programmer was less than remorseful. "That's all to be expected."

"To be expected!? We paid good money for this!"

"Of course. It's a good program. It was a very difficult program to write. Why do you think it should be easy to understand?"

The boss found himself stymied several times a day by the computer error message "FILE NOT FOUND." The fact that he might be typing the filename incorrectly never occurred to him.

Infuriated, he summoned the firm's part-time techie to his office. "Fix it!" he demanded. "I don't care how you do it. Just fix it."

Next day about mid-morning, he tried to access a word processing file and was greeted with this cheery memo onscreen: "Hi! The file you requested apparently has been pilfered by a subordinate for no good reason. You really should investigate and show this person who's boss. However, for the time being, you might prefer to simply CLICK HERE and choose from a long, long list of filename alternatives."

• • • •

Cyberlaw #1: "ASCII stupid question,
get a stupid ANSI."
Cyberlaw #2: "All computers wait
at precisely the same speed."

• • • •

How long is a computer's attention span?
As long as its power cord.

• • • •

Computers do make mistakes—
and they make them very quickly.

• • • •

Final instruction in a computer manual: "If all else fails,
pound fist on keyboard to continue."

An accountant was startled when this message popped up on his computer monitor: "As a computer, I find your dependency on automation highly amusing."

# CROOKS

Judge: "Don't you want a lawyer to represent you?"
Defendant: "Naw, I've decided to tell the truth."

• • • •

Did you hear about the Most Wanted Man who was so bad he shot at people with a bitten-off shotgun?

• • • •

Two prisoners were commiserating. "What are you in here for?" asked one.

"Stealing a truckload of cement."

"Catch you red-handed?"

"Yeah, the evidence was pretty concrete."

• • • •

A small boy went with his mother to the Post Office and was curious about the wanted posters on display.

"Those are people the police are trying to catch for committing awful crimes," his mother explained.

"Well, why didn't the police just keep them when they took those pictures?"

A group of baseball players were commiserating after a game. "Can you believe it?" one player said to the others. "We paid the ump $100 in advance to give us the game, and he let us lose anyway."

"Some umpires are thieves," consoled his friends.

• • • •

A policeman was interrogating two suspects. "Where do you live?" he asked the first.

"No permanent address."

"What about you?" the policeman asked the second.

"Next-door to him."

# DATING

A heartsick teen-age boy tagged along with the girl of his dreams in the school hallway between classes.

"You never tell me what's on your mind," he whined.

"What would be the point? None of it has anything to do with you."

• • • •

"I don't reckon Margaret and I will ever get married," lamented Fred.

"Why not?" asked a friend.

"Well, she likes to argue all the time—and I don't even like to talk much."

• • • •

How do you repair a heartbreak?
With ticker-tape.

A young couple went to see a premarital counselor. They were both very nervous as the counselor began taking notes.

"Your name?" the counselor asked the man.

"Williams," the man replied.

"And your first name?"

"Ah, John. It's John. John Williams."

"I see. And your fiancé's name?"

"Barker."

"Her first name?"

"Oh, heavens! I can't remember it. Mary, please tell the counselor your first name."

• • • •

A city family on vacation in the mountains sat on the porch of a local family, enthralled by the humorous, tragic, and adventurous stories of bygone hillfolk. One tale involved a distant cousin who eloped with her beau.

"Yep," the patriarch of the mountain clan said, "they just walked right up that mountain there, never looked behind 'em and never came back down here."

"Well, what happened to them?" asked the city man.

"Walked down the other side to Mayville, I expect."

• • • •

On the first day of classes, a brash young college boy asked the pretty girl seated next to him for her phone number.

"It's in the phone book," she told him coyly.

"Under what name?" he pressed.

"That's in the book, too."

A teen-age couple at a movie theater were more than conspicuous with their audible running commentary about the acting and the plot. At length, a woman seated behind them tapped the boy on the shoulder. "Do you want us to ask them to turn down the volume of the movie so you can hear each other more clearly?"

• • • •

"The difference between dating and marrying," a father advised his college son, "is a matter of expectations."

"What do you mean, Dad?"

"You take your girl out to dinner, for example. She appreciates it. You take your wife out to dinner—she expects it."

• • • •

Three eligible widows were discussing several eligible widowers in their church.

"Now George is a nice man," remarked one, "and he really doesn't look 60."

Another was far less impressed by George's youthful appearance. "Well," she said, "he used to look 60."

• • • •

Henry knelt in front of his girl Henrietta and pleaded, "I've told you before and I'll tell you again: I just can't live without you."

"Yeah, I heard you the first time, and all the other times," she replied. "I would think you'd be dead by now."

A grizzled old mountain man knocked on the town doctor's door late one night. The doctor and his wife came to the door and were shocked to see that the mountaineer supported a blood-stained teen-ager.

"Sew 'im up real good, Doc," the mountaineer said, dragging the young man inside. "He's my son-in-law. I shot 'im myself, I'm afeared."

"Why in the world," shouted the doctor, scrambling for his bag, "did you shoot your own son-in-law?"

"Well, he warn't my son-in-law when I shot 'im. He warn't my son-in-law 'til an hour or two ago when I caught 'im kissin' my Millie out on the porch."

• • • •

Robert was explaining to a friend a problem that had arisen in his relationship with Megan. "We have a strong disagreement over our wedding plans," he said.

"She probably wants it to be a big, expensive affair," guessed the friend.

"Not exactly. I keep telling her a small garden wedding would be nice, and she keeps telling me we should start dating other people."

# DEFINITIONS

advertisement: *a photo or video of an attractive man or woman driving, drinking, eating, wearing, or doing something no one really needs.*

alibi: *legal proof that a person was not where he or she really was.*

ambiguity: *telling the truth accidentally.*

ambush: *the way a shrub introduces itself to a tree.*

appeal: *the protective covering of a banana.*

assault: *the condiment that complements apepper.*

axiom: *something that's so clear there's no need to see it.*

bachelor: *husband of a spinster.*

bacteria: *the rear entrance of a cafeteria.*

bank: *a place where you can borrow money—provided you can prove you don't need to.*

best man: *the one the bride doesn't marry.*

birth-resurrectionist: *a person who attends church only at Christmas and Easter.*

blood vessel: *a hospital ship.*

budget: *a plan for systematically going broke.*

budget: *the practice of applied worrying both before and after you spend money.*

Cheerios: *doughnut seeds.*

committee: *a group of people whose purpose is to divide responsibility and put off action for as long as possible.*

computer programmer: *a happy-go-lucky human trained to consume seven pizzas a week and interrupt perfectly normal conversations to consult aloud with imaginary colleagues.*

contralto: *a low form of music, usually sung by women.*

depressed: *a bankrupt dry cleaner.*

dilate: *to live to a ripe old age.*

diplomacy: *the art of saying "Nice dog!" until you can get your hands on a stick.*

diplomacy: *the art of letting someone else have your own way.*

Dodgers: *jaywalkers in LA.*

dogma: *mother of a collie pup.*

duffer: *a golfing enthusiast who shouts "Fore!," takes 5 strokes, then writes 3 on the scorecard.*

Eskimos: *God's frozen people.*

experience: *another word for "mistakes."*

failure: *the road of least persistence.*

fingerprints: *all that's left in the refrigerator 30 minutes after your children pile in from school.*

germinate: *to be born in Germany.*

goblet: *a small turkey.*

gossip: *a mouth trap.*

gossiper: *someone with a lively sense of rumor.*

graffiti: *the writing on the mall wall.*

Grand Prix racing: *trying to reach the phone before your teen-age daughter.*

gruesome: *one of the things your child did at summer camp.*

horse sense: *stable thinking.*

humanitarian: *a person who eats only people.*

hypnotism: *rheumatism in the hip.*

impeccable: *something a chicken can't eat.*

infinity: *the knowledge that if you had everything, you would have no place to keep it all.*

instinct: *a skunk's defense mechanism.*

invoice: *another word for "conscience."*

invoice: *the only voice some people have in their spouse's buying decisions.*

lightyear: *365 days with only 365 calories a day.*

minority rule: *a newborn baby just home from the hospital.*

miracle workers: *lazy employees (it's a miracle when they work).*

mistake: *Mr. Take's wife.*

monologue: *a conversation between a politician and somebody else.*

musical interval: *the distance between two pianos.*

myth: *a girl moth.*

offshore drillers: *Navy dentists.*

optimist: *a person with limited experience.*

optimist: *a person who marries a pessimist.*

overbite: *an affliction suffered by fat people.*

parking place: *a place occupied by somebody else's vehicle.*

perfect pitch: *a string bass being thrown into a dumpster without touching the sides.*

perfectionist: *a person who goes to infinite pains and spreads them to the people nearby.*

pessimist: *a person who carries a wallet card that reads, "in case of accident: I always knew it would happen sooner or later."*

pro football coach: *a man who's willing to lay down his players' lives in order to win.*

psychiatry: *one profession in which the customer is always wrong.*

punchbowl: *a boxing arena.*

puncture: *a very short slit in a tire a very long way from home.*

quarterback: *a nominal refund.*

refugee: *an official at a professional wrestling match.*

resurrection workers: *employees who come to life at 5 p.m.*

righteous indignation: *getting angry but not swearing.*

rotisserie: *a Ferris wheel for dead chickens.*

sailing: *the sport of idling around in circles while you get wet and catch a cold.*

secret: *something you're supposed to tell only one listener at a time.*

shin: *the human bone most useful for finding hard obstacles in the dark.*

smile: *a device for improving face value.*

sneeze: *eruption of a tickle in the throat.*

specialist: *a meticulously trained professional who knows more and more about less and less;* medical specialist: *a doctor who prefers a smaller practice and a larger house.*

stockholder: *the cowboy who keeps the chute closed while waiting for the starting signal at a rodeo.*

synonym: *a good word to use if you can't think of the right word.*

TLC: *"takes a lot of cash."*

upgrade: *a computer program with new and improved bugs.*

Victorian Era: *Queen Victoria's mistaken reign.*

war department: *the church music committee.*

yardstick: *a boomerang that doesn't return.*

# DENTISTS

Patient: "So how do my teeth check out?"
Doctor: "Oh, they're lovely. We're going to have to remove some gums, though."

. . . .

His jaw throbbing, a man with an abscessed tooth phoned the dentist's office.

"We can see you on the 19th," suggested the receptionist.

"I might die of pain by then!"

"Well, in that situation, simply arrange for someone to phone and cancel the appointment."

. . . .

The dentist was straightforward with his patient. "Now, this may hurt a bit. We're going to have to give you a shot of local anesthesia."

The patient took the shot in stride, and after the anesthesia had taken effect, the dentist began to drill. Later, job done, he let the patient out of the chair.

The patient turned before leaving and remarked, "Now, this may hurt a bit. I don't have the money to pay. . . ."

# DIETING

Two jocks were taking a break in the gym.
  "What's your weight?"
  "About 190."
  "Gained a little, haven't you?"
  "More'n a little. I only weighed 8 pounds 5 ounces when I was born."

• • • •

Lill: "I just finished a three-month diet."
Janny: "What did you lose?"
Lill: "Three months of good eating."

• • • •

"Wow, you've lost a lot of weight. You look great!"
  "New diet."
  "Really? What can you eat?"
  "I can eat absolutely anything I want, any time of day. I'm just not allowed to swallow it."

• • • •

A man came home from the doctor's office, and his wife asked how he had checked out.
  "Hmph," the man said disgustedly. "He told me I'm either 40 pounds too heavy or 4 inches too short."

A hefty gentleman stepped onto a pay scale and put in a dime. He was not amused when the machine registered this message: "ONE CUSTOMER PER DIME."

• • • •

A beggar approached a lady on the street and pleaded, "Ma'am, I haven't had a meal in three days, and—"

"Now, that," she interrupted, "is what I call willpower."

• • • •

A little boy was giving his friend a tour of his house. "And this is our bathroom scale," he pointed out.

The guest had never seen a scale before. "What's it for?" he inquired.

"I don't know, but when grown-ups stand on it, it makes 'em real mad."

• • • •

Two vastly overweight people were waxing jealous of acquaintances of slighter stature.

"Take Harrison, for example," said one. "She's so thin, if she sat down on a nickel, four cents would be exposed."

• • • •

Marie: "I've figured out a way to lose almost a quarter of your body weight instantly."

Charlie: "Tell me how."

Marie: "Just have them amputate one of your legs."

# DINING IN, DINING OUT

The restaurant's claim to fame was that it offered every kind of dish you could think of.

"Tiger steak, basted in Worcestershire sauce, medium rare," ordered one challenger.

The waiter returned in a few minutes and reported, "You'll have to try something else. We're out of Worcestershire sauce tonight."

● ● ● ●

Waitress: "And how did you find your sautéed shrimp tonight?"

Diner: "Quite by accident. I finished the last of the veggies and discovered all three shrimp had been right there the whole time."

● ● ● ●

Jones: "My wife prepared an Italian meal last night, with recipes from a real Italian cookbook."

James: "I didn't know she could read Italian."

Jones: "She can't. Can't cook it, either."

● ● ● ●

Diner: "Are you sure this is blueberry pie? It tastes like cardboard."

Waiter: "Yep, that would be the blueberry. The strawberry pie tastes like adhesive tape."

"Mom, don't I have a choice for dinner?" tested Nathan.

"Of course, dear. You can either eat it or go to bed hungry."

• • • •

A woman sat down at a lunch counter, gestured to the beverage section of the menu board and told the waitress, "I'll have a free refill of coffee with cream and artificial sweetener."

• • • •

Name of a 24-hour oriental restaurant:
"Wok 'Round the Clock."

• • • •

Shopper: "I can't find the wild rice."
Grocer: "We're out. But we can shake up a box of tame rice and at least make it mad."

• • • •

"I don't understand how to figure these recipes," Julie complained. "They're all written to serve four, and we're having 12 for dinner Saturday."

"Oh, you simply triple everything," her mother explained.

Julie frowned. "But our oven doesn't go up to 900 degrees."

• • • •

What's a cannibal's favorite dinner?
Baked bein's.

It was closing time on Thanksgiving Eve, and the supermarket meat department was predictably devoid of turkeys.

"Oh, no! Have you none left at all?" wailed a belated shopper rushing to the meat counter. "I've got 11 people coming for dinner tomorrow."

There was, in fact, one bird left—the one the butcher had sequestered in a corner of the back freezer for his own consumption. Feeling pity for the unprepared hostess, he offered to sell it to her.

"Oh, it's rather small," she whined. "Won't you please see if there is anything else?"

Chagrined, the butcher returned the turkey to the back room, mounted it on a smaller frame, then took it back outside to the counter. "What about this one?"

The ruse worked. "Yes," beamed the shopper, "that one's obviously larger. Now let me buy them both, and I'll be just fine."

• • • •

A gentleman on his way to the bathroom at a restaurant crunched the foot of a woman sitting at a nearby table. He didn't bother to stop and apologize.

A few minutes later he returned, winding his way through the crowded dining room. Passing the same woman's table, he stopped. "Did I step on your toe a little while ago?"

"I'm afraid so."

"Good," he said. "That means I'm on the right course back."

• • • •

Paper-clipped special in a lunch menu: SOUTHERN STYLE MANHATTAN CLAM CHOWDER.

Janice, retired, dearly enjoyed serving several days a week at her church's soup kitchen. Sometimes it meant her husband had to fix his own lunch at home alone.

"You prepare more food for strangers than you do for me," he grumbled.

"But they," she rejoined, "never complain about the cooking."

• • • •

Two strangers leaving a large restaurant happened to arrive at the coat rack simultaneously.

"Are you William Morrison from San Antonio?" asked one.

"No," was the curt reply.

"Well, I am, and you just put on his overcoat."

• • • •

In one part of the jungle is a strangely religious tribe of cannibals. On Fridays they eat only fishermen.

• • • •

Randy, a big, strapping fellow, spends his Saturdays doing yard work for elderly folks around the community. His wages are simple: "I tell them they can pay me or they can feed me."

One woman thought the latter would be a wonderful deal, especially since she loved to impress folks with her kitchen talents. At the end of his work day, she sat him down to a steaming, delicious plate of home cooking, which he quickly devoured. Taking his hint, she served seconds. . .then thirds. It seemed the more food she offered, the hungrier he was.

A week or two later, at the conclusion of his work day she met him at the door—checkbook in hand.

# DOCTORS & PATIENTS

The emergency room victim was a worker who had fallen from a fifth-floor window. Amazingly, the man was still conscious and, in fact, seemed to be only mildly affected by the accident. While they waited for X-ray results, an ER staffer gathered information for the record.

"And where do you work?" came the question.

"I used to work for EFG Construction," the patient replied.

"How long since you left that job?"

"Since about half-way to the ground."

• • • •

"Did you read in the paper today about the suicide doctor who's vowed to give it all up?" asked Pastor Becker.

"You mean, he's finally seen the light?" asked Pastor Shelby.

"Well, not exactly. It seems the pill he prescribed failed to work, by the grace of God—and now he's being sued for medical malpractice."

• • • •

"I really appreciate you coming out to our house this late at night," remarked a sick patient.

"No problem," said the doctor. "I had to come see Mr. Oaks just down the road, anyway. This way I can kill two birds with one stone."

A patient braced himself as the doctor entered the examining room after obtaining X-rays. "Is there any hope at all?" the patient asked.

"That depends," the doctor replied, "on what you're hoping for."

• • • •

A surgeon was surrounded by admirers at a party, and during the course of the conversation, one gentleman asked eruditely, "Dr. Smurthwaite, what specific segment of the typical surgical procedure do you find least enjoyable?"

The good doctor smiled. "Threading the needle."

• • • •

Why do doctors wear white masks during surgery?
So no one will be sure who to blame.

• • • •

Arnie: "I just got a new lease on life."
Barney: "How's that?"
Arnie: "Well, you know my doctor told me I had six months to live."
Barney: "No! I hadn't heard that."
Arnie: "Yeah. But I couldn't afford to pay his bill. So today, he told me I have six more months."

• • • •

Why is it that it takes a pain reliever less time to act than it takes the consumer to figure out how to open the bottle?

A patient told his doctor, "My wife always has complained about my snoring, but I never took her seriously. Now, though, I realize she was right. As I get older, I'm beginning to wake myself up with my own snoring. What can I do?"

"Sleep in a different room," advised the doctor.

• • • •

"Doc, it's the wooden leg," complained a patient. "It's a terrible pain."

"Is the fit uncomfortable?" queried the doctor.

"Oh, no. It's the wife. At night when I take the leg off, she bangs me over the head with it."

• • • •

"You're extremely ill," the doctor admonished a patient. "Why didn't you come to me yesterday?"

"Well, I wanted to give myself a chance to get well, first."

• • • •

A brawny construction worker fell from a building and was rushed to the hospital with a dislocated shoulder. The hospital was very crowded, and he ended up in the maternity ward. His pain was tremendous, even with a sedative, and he screamed uncontrollably.

"Shhhh," admonished a nurse. "The women in the adjoining rooms have all been through childbirth, and despite their agony, none of them made as much racket as you."

"No?" shrieked the worker. "See how they sound if you try to relocate their babies."

A doctor remarked to a colleague, "You look worried today. What's on your mind?"

"New patient," was the reply. "I always worry about this type."

"What's the medical history? Cancer?"

"No. Malpractice suits."

• • • •

"I'm afraid you're going to have to give up every form of dessert," the doctor told Mrs. Stewart. "You're simply overweight, and that's the best advice I can give you."

Mrs. Stewart considered a moment. "And what's your second-best advice?"

• • • •

Patient: "My head feels like iron, my neck is stiff as a lead pipe and my nose is completely stopped."
Doctor: "Sounds like you need a plumber, not a doctor."

• • • •

An irate woman phoned her doctor's office. "I just received your bill for my visit last week. You charged me $120!"

The receptionist pulled the record up on the computer screen. "That's correct, Mrs. Adams. $120."

"But all he did was paint my throat!"

"That's correct. Wallpaper costs $150."

• • • •

"He's shot bad," remarked one emergency medical technician to another as they struggled to staunch the bleeding of a gangster lying on the street.

The patient opened his eyes and glared at the EMT. "What's it like to be shot good?"

"They say medical procedures are far more advanced today than they were a quarter of a century ago," a woman commented to a friend. "So why is it that after all these expensive procedures, I feel so much worse than I felt back then?"

• • • •

A resident doctor was analyzing a set of X-rays with an intern. "You can see that my patient's left lung is collapsed. That's why she wheezes constantly. Now, what would you do in this case?"

"I reckon I'd be wheezing, too."

• • • •

Doctor: "I'm afraid you have a dangerously advanced case of bronchitis."
Patient: "I only had the sniffles when I first sat down in your waiting room."

• • • •

What's the first thing they teach medical students?

"Prescriptions may be scribbled. Billing statements always should be typed."

• • • •

A patient was having her first consultation with a prospective surgeon. "How long have you been in practice?" the patient asked.

"It's been almost a year since I completed my residency."

"Keep practicing," she said, showing herself to the door.

"We're just going to apply a local anesthetic now," the anesthesiologist gently explained to the surgical patient.

"Don't spare the expense!" barked the patient. "Give me an import!"

• • • •

Dr. James wasn't at all pleased to discover Mrs. Bryan had come to him for a third opinion before agreeing to surgery. "You should have come to me to begin with," he stated. "Who did you see first?"

"Dr. Morgan."

"Well, I suppose there are worse GPs, but the man has no vision. What did he tell you?"

"He said I need surgery, but I should get another doctor's opinion."

"And who did you see next?"

"Dr. Lattimore."

"The imbecile! That man's knowledge of medicine could be contained in a thimble. His advice is totally worthless. What on earth did he tell you?"

"He told me to come see you."

• • • •

"Can you do anything to keep my ears from ringing?" asked a patient.

"Hmm. Have you considered getting an unlisted head?"

• • • •

"Is there anything I can do to preserve my hair?" a patient asked.

"No," said the doctor, "but we may be able to shrink your head so that the hair you have fits better."

"Why don't you go to a doctor?" Mrs. Ward suggested to her friend.

"Why should I?" asked Mrs. Richardson. "There's nothing at all wrong with me."

"Oh, these doctors today," marveled Mrs. Ward, "they're so good, they'll find something wrong with you."

• • • •

Pharmacist: "Wow, Mr. Kettle, it's been a long time since you came in for a refill of this prescription. Have you been taking one pill three times a day, as instructed?"

Mr. Kettle: "Well, I tried that, son. But I found out that once you take a pill the first time, it's slap gone."

• • • •

"So how are we feeling today?" cheerily asked the doctor as she checked in on an intensive care patient.

"Ong. . .wheeze. . .gettashungtaboo!"

The doctor leaned closer. "What did you say?"

"Yershtoba. . .agh. . .tubaflor!"

The doc proffered her notepad. "Why don't you write it for me. I can't understand what you're saying."

The patient wrote: "Get your foot off the oxygen tube!!!"

• • • •

"My nose is too long," the man informed the plastic surgeon. "What will it take to shorten it?"

"About $5,000—and the pain will be considerable."

"I can bear the pain, but I can't bear the fee. Are there alternatives?"

"You might consider using the side of this brick building."

A doctor was weary of being asked for medical opinions everywhere he went, especially in social settings. Once at a church supper, a deacon diverted a casual conversation to describe certain pains that had been bothering him as he entered middle age. "I'd really like to know if this indicates a liver problem," the deacon hinted, looking at the doctor questioningly.

The doctor answered coldly. "Well, we certainly should see. Undress right here, and I'll perform an examination."

Word got around. The doctor was never badgered again.

• • • •

"The odds are good," the doctor informed Throckmorton, discussing his impending surgery. "Three out of four patients come through this with no permanent debilities."

"And how have your last three patients fared?" Throckmorton was keen to know.

• • • •

"A hot compress," the doctor advised after examining the huge knot on the head of a patient. "That will make the swelling go down."

The patient went home and applied a hot compress, but after a few hours it obviously was doing no good. The patient's wife came home, sized up the situation and shook her head. "You need a cold compress," she stated, and proceeded to apply one to the wound. Sure enough, within an hour the knot had vanished.

The next day, the patient phoned his doctor to point out that his wife's prescription for a cold compress had succeeded whereas the doctor's advice had failed. The doctor shrugged. "Hot water, cold water? My wife tells me to use hot."

Why did the surgeon wear a tuxedo in the OR?
He preferred formal openings.

• • • •

A man was taken to the hospital emergency room suffering agonizing stomach pains.
"What did you eat last?" asked the ER physician.
"Pecans."
"Roasted or plain?"
"Got no idea. They were still inside the shells."

• • • •

A particularly garrulous patient was about to drive his doctor nuts during an examination. At length, the doctor instructed, "Now hold your tongue between your fingers, please."
When he did so, the doctor placed a not-unpleasant drop of medicine on the top of the tongue. "Hold it until the medicine dissolves," he told the patient.
While the patient held his tongue, the doctor wrote out several prescriptions. When the patient had left, the nurse commented, "That was merely a glucose solution in the medicine dropper. Why did you give him that?"
"I had to shut him up so I could think."

• • • •

"Doctor, my husband thinks he's a bubblegum machine. What can I do?"
"Bring him in and I'll ask him some questions."
"Okay. . .but can we pay you in nickels?"

The patient looked suspicious when the nurse came in with his medicine.

"And how are we feeling today?" the surgeon asked with a smile as the patient was wheeled into the operating room.

"Fine, but a little nervous," the patient said. "This is my first operation."

"I know the feeling. It's my first operation, too."

• • • •

An ear doctor was raving to a patient about the extraordinary powers of a new hearing device. "I wear it myself, and I swear I can hear even better now than normal folks can hear."

"Oh, really? What kind is it?"

"About 11:20, I think."

• • • •

"How did it go with Mr. Smollett's appendectomy?" asked Dr. George.

Dr. Cline looked confused. "Appendectomy? Did you say appendectomy?"

"Yes. Mr. Smollett's."

"Heaven forbid!" cried Dr. Cline. "I thought they ordered an autopsy on Mr. Smollett!"

• • • •

A surgeon asked a patient, "Could you afford an operation if I thought it was necessary?"

The patient replied, "Would you think it was necessary if I couldn't afford one?"

Nurse: "Your cough seems more relaxed this morning."
Sleepless patient: "I guess practice makes perfect."

• • • •

A couple included their doctor and his wife on an invitation list for a dinner party. When a scribbled note arrived in the mail from the doctor's office, they pondered it at length.

"I really can't tell if it's an acceptance or if he's sending their regrets."

"Neither can I," said her husband. Then a happy thought occurred to him. "Why don't we take it to the pharmacy? They can read any doctor's handwriting there."

To the pharmacy they went. The pharmacist scrutinized the note, then went into a back room. He returned in a few minutes with a vial of pills. "Sixty-three dollars," he said.

• • • •

"Doc, I don't think I'm feeling too well," said an agitated man, barging into the room.

"I should say not," said a man in a white jacket. "I'm a chef. This is a restaurant."

• • • •

A doctor stepped in to report to a patient after analyzing the results of an examination. He looked very concerned.

"Don't give me any bad news," the patient ordered. "I can't afford surgery and I'm not ready to die."

"Perfect! I've got another patient looking for an excuse to get out of work. I'll just switch your X-rays with his."

Caller: "I need to be tested. I've noticed a deterioration in my short-term memory."
Receptionist: "You'll have to pay in advance."

• • • •

The patient looked suspicious when the nurse came in with his medicine.

"You're sure this is my medicine?" he quizzed. "I'm Blalock, here with a liver condition."

"Oh, yes sir," humored the nurse. "You're Mr. Blalock, Room 302, and you're supposed to take this three times a day for your liver."

"Forgive my caution," Mr. Blalock apologized, "but I've heard of patients dying because their medicine was accidentally switched."

The nurse beamed. "Don't worry. If you come here with a liver problem, you die with a liver problem."

• • • •

The prognosis was simple: The patient had a head cold. "There's still no cure for the common cold," the doctor sighed. "Just take aspirin, drink lots of liquids and rest in bed."

"But Doc, I'm miserable. You've gotta recommend some kinda cure."

The doctor was thoughtful a moment. "I'll tell you what. Why don't you take off your coat and shoes and hike up the mountain outside town?"

"Are you crazy? There's a snowstorm out there! I'll get pneumonia!"

"Yes. That I can cure."

# ECONOMICS

Farmer Adams was bragging to farmer Black. "I really had a fine day at the market. Guess how many watermelons I sold?"

"'Bout half, I s'ppose."

"Half? Half what?"

"Half as many as you're about to claim."

• • • •

Sign in a department store window in May: ONLY 224 SHOPPING DAYS LEFT UNTIL CHRISTMAS!

• • • •

"Always live within your means," a tax consultant advised a client.

"Oh, we do," responded the client. "We just have to take out loans in order to do it."

• • • •

It was the late Senator Everett Dirksen who quipped, "A billion here, a billion there. . . . Pretty soon, you're talking about real money."

• • • •

Passerby: "You should be ashamed, sitting on the street begging."

Sidewalk beggar: "I'm truly sorry, but I can't afford to open an office."

Hats were advertised at the department store at $10 each or two for $15. A man approached the counter with two in his hands.

"Now, if I just buy this one, how much will it cost me?"

"That one by itself will cost $10, as marked," the clerk determined.

"And if I buy them both?"

"You can have them both for $15 total."

"Well, I'll just take the $5 one."

• • • •

"Do you have a card?" one businesswoman asked another.

Cards were exchanged, and the first woman looked puzzled. "There's no name on it."

The second woman glanced around furtively. "That's for tax purposes. I need to maintain my anonymity."

• • • •

A man was shopping for a portable CD player at a discount store. "You're asking $89.95," he told the electronics clerk. "Your competitor is advertising this same brand, same model, for $69.95."

"So why don't you go over there and buy one?"

"I phoned. They're out."

"Yeah. When we were out," the clerk said, "we had 'em marked down to 70 bucks, too."

• • • •

Amanda: "Daddy, does money really talk?"

"No, honey. It goes without saying."

"You look really down."

"I am down. Nothing's going right."

"Try to focus on the positive things in your life. You have a beautiful wife, smart children, you just moved into a big new house, you drive a BMW and own a luxury sailboat, and you've started a new job."

"The job—I think that's the problem. It only pays $55 a week."

• • • •

"We were so poor when I was growing up," exclaimed old Ned, "I didn't get to celebrate my 6th birthday until I was 18."

• • • •

Amid the happy conversation of a luncheonette at mid-day, a man suddenly cried out, "My son's choking! He's swallowed a quarter! Help! Please, anyone! Help!"

A man from the adjoining dining room heard the cries, rushed in, seized the child bodily and gave a sudden squeeze around the midriff. The child coughed up the quarter and went back to eating as though nothing had happened.

"Thank you! Thank you!" cried the father. "Are you a paramedic?"

"No," replied the rescuer. "I work for the IRS."

• • • •

"We're a bit short this month," said Mr. Bentley with a frown. "Won't have enough to pay the water bill."

Mrs. Bentley frowned, too—until a happy thought occurred to her. "Well, we won't have to worry about that leaky toilet bowl for awhile!"

A millionaire's small daughter was asked to write an essay in school about the poor. Her piece went like this:

"Once upon a time there was a poor man. He lived in a lonely part of town. His wife was as poor as he was. So was their butler. So were their maids. So was the gardener. So was the chef. . . ."

• • • •

One tax planner was so brilliant her clients lobbied to have a loophole named after her.

# GOVERNMENT

Have you heard about the new short form for income tax returns? It reads:
1) How much money do you earn?
2) Send it to us.

• • • •

The town council of a rapidly growing metropolis was overwhelmed with complaints from citizens concerning the plethora of potholes caused by heavy construction vehicles.

"Should we hire more staff to handle the calls?" asked the town manager.

"No, get an unlisted number," said the mayor.

• • • •

President Calvin Coolidge, when pressed by a reporter as to why he was declining to seek reelection, replied, "No chance for advancement."

A woman had been waiting in line more than an hour at the tax office. "If they didn't give us so much red tape to go through," she fumed to no one in particular, "both the government and the taxpayers would be better off."

A bedraggled clerk overheard the remark and snapped, "If we want your opinion, we will provide you with the appropriate form to complete."

• • • •

A cave man explained to his clan the reasons they needed to establish an elected government. The tribe listened patiently as he talked. Then another man stood up.

"Let me get this straight," he said. "You want me and the other guys to go out every day, hunt dangerous mastodons and sabre-toothed tigers while you sleep late inside the cave, give you part of the food, let you dictate to us where and when we're entitled to hunt—and this is for the good of us all?"

• • • •

A secret agent was directed to a posh condominium complex to contact an anonymous source. "Williams is the name," he was told by his superior. "Hand him this envelope."

Arriving at the complex, he was confused to find four different Williamses occupying adjacent quarters. He decided to try the second condo. When a gentleman answered his knock, the agent spoke the pass code: "The grape arbor is down."

Looking him over, the man shook his head. "I'm Williams the accountant. You might try Williams the spy. Two doors down."

A dying man told his wife he wanted to join the Democratic Party. All his life he'd been a Republican, and his wife wondered why he felt the sudden change in political bent in his final days. His logic: "I want it to be them losing a voter, not us."

• • • •

Two men were waiting in line at the clerk of court's office.

"Title research?" asked one.

"Nah. Changin' my name."

"Really? And what's your name, if I might ask?"

"Arnie Goobomalong."

"Ummm. I can see why you'd want to change that. So what'll be your new name?"

"Jerry Goobomalong."

# HEADLINES & NEWS NOTES

SUSPECT SAYS HE FIRED GUN TO FRIGHTEN DECEASED

• • • •

ELDERLY MAN SLIPS IN BATHTUB,
BREAKS NEW YEAR'S RESOLUTION

• • • •

CARS COLLIDE; ONE CHARGE WITH ABUSIVE LANGUAGE

• • • •

CAR HITS JAYWALKER WITH NO HEADLIGHTS

"If across-the-board salary raises are not approved for District Five teachers, several have threatened to abandon their pests."

• • • •

"The refreshment table was superintended by Mrs. Smith, overflowing with sweets and sandwiches."

• • • •

WOMAN EXPECTED TO RECOVER FROM FATAL CRASH

• • • •

SHORTAGE OF BRAINS HAMPERS RESEARCH

• • • •

RASH OF ACCIDENTS KEEPS EMT CREWS HOPPING

• • • •

BUS STRIKES MAN, DECLINES ASSISTANCE

• • • •

AIRPLANE HITS THREE HOUSES, KILLS TWO

• • • •

DINNER THEATER RELIES ON SEASONED CAST

• • • •

SUSPECT WOUNDS WRONG WIFE,
SAYS HE'S SORRY

• • • •

SLAIN YOUTH FOUND ALIVE

# HUNTING & FISHING

Old Bart, the best hunter in the county, had the questionable privilege of taking his new preacher bird hunting one Saturday afternoon. Later, taking his ease with a cup of coffee beside the pot-bellied stove at the crossroads store, he was asked by the other regulars about the preacher's prowess with a shotgun.

"Well, I can't tell you no lie," Bart said. "He's a right decent shot. But it sure was somethin' to behold the way the Lord protected those birds."

• • • •

A group of buddies rented a wilderness lodge for a week of hunting in the mountains. Walking onto the porch one morning after an early breakfast, they found an old man rocking in the chair.

"Be rainin' by mid-day," he prophesied.

Sure enough, after a few hours in the woods they were caught in a heavy rainstorm.

The next morning when they went outside, the old man again was in his rocker.

"Think it'll rain today, pop?" one of the hunters asked.

"Nope. Fair all day. A mite chilly, though."

The weather was fair and chilly, indeed. And each day thereafter, the ancient prognosticator's weather forecast held true.

On the final day of their vacation, the hunters hurried onto the porch, eager to hear the old-timer's prediction. "What'll the weather be today?" one asked.

The local shook his head. "Dunno. My radio's broke."

Three statisticians were duck hunting. A duck flew across the pond in front of their blind. One statistician fired, but the shot passed just ahead of the duck. The second statistician's shot passed just behind. The third announced, "We got him!"

• • • •

The hunter from the East had paid top dollar for his guide. At the end of a day, not only had they found no moose; it was obvious by their vague course and the guide's worried countenance that they were lost.

"You're supposed to be the best guide in Montana," the hunter fumed.

"Yep. I think we're in Canada, though."

• • • •

An old-timer joined a deer hunt and was quite the center of attention as the others watched him prime his muzzle-loader. Remarkably, after he loaded the gunpowder, he sprinkled in a good helping of salt.

"Now, what's the salt for?" asked one observer.

"I expect to be shootin' from a fur piece, nigh onto a mile," the crusty hunter answered. "Don't want the buck to spoil afore I kin git to 'im."

• • • •

A couple walking home from church met a little boy with a fishing pole over his shoulder, a modest string of fish in one hand and an empty bait bucket in the other.

"The Good Book," the man admonished, "says the Sabbath should be a holy day."

"Yessir," the boy responded. "I'm punishing these fish for eating all my worms on Sunday."

# HUSBANDS & WIVES

Dad and Junior had been fishing when they should have been tending to the chores Mom had outlined on Saturday morning. When she discovered their laziness at the end of the day, she was furious. She followed them around the house, shouting.

At length, the father pulled his son inside the foyer closet and locked the door. His wife pounded on the door. "Come out of there, you two!"

"No!" came the muffled response.

"Come out right now!"

"We will not!" the husband insisted. He turned to his son in the darkness. "Guess I showed her who's boss in this house."

• • • •

"I heard you and your wife arguing last night," a man remarked to his neighbor, a newlywed. "Honeymoon over?"

"Not really. It's just that when it comes to some things, I won't change my opinion and she won't change the subject."

• • • •

A man was arguing with his wife over which sex (male or female) shows better judgment. Ultimately, she gave in. "You're right. Men exercise better judgment, and the two of us are living proof of it, aren't we? I mean, you chose me for a wife, and I chose you for a husband."

• • • •

Mrs. Laird: "Do you ever wake up grouchy in the morning?"
Mrs. Baird: "No, I usually let him just get up whenever he's ready."

A young couple were looking to buy their first home. "It may not work for us yet," the woman told the realtor candidly. "We have a very limited budget."

"Well, just tell me what price you think you can afford," the realtor said cheerily. "We'll all enjoy the laugh and then get down to serious business."

• • • •

The hot topic of conversation at the Hollywood wedding reception was the fact that it was the bride's eighth marriage. Mused one gossip columnist to another, "They say she has a mania for wedding cake."

• • • •

On their anniversary night, the husband sat his wife down in the den with her favorite magazine, turned on the soft reading lamp, slipped off her shoes, patted and propped up her feet and announced he was preparing dinner all by himself. "How romantic!" she thought.

Two-and-a-half hours later she was still waiting for dinner to be served. She tip-toed to the kitchen and found it a colossal mess. Her harried husband, removing something indescribable from the smoking oven, saw her in the doorway.

"Almost ready!" he vowed. "Sorry it took me so long— I had to refill the pepper shaker."

"Why, Honey, how long could that have taken you?"

"More'n an hour, I reckon. Wasn't easy stuffin' it through those dumb little holes."

• • • •

Husband: "I'm sorry if I don't always seem to be paying attention to you, dear."
Wife: "That's all right. I knew when I married you that you were hard of listening."

A man came home after a terrible day at work and was disappointed that his wife, equally worn out, hardly spoke a word.

"Well," he prodded. "Aren't you going to ask me what kind of day I had?"

"I'm sorry—of course. How was it at the office?"

"Please. Don't ask. . . ."

• • • •

A man and his wife were browsing through the men's section of a department store. Absentmindedly flipping through neckties, the man turned to his wife and asked, "Honey, do I like this one?"

• • • •

A man had dinner waiting when his wife came home one evening. "I've cooked my two specialties," he said, sitting her down. "Lasagna and pecan pie, just for you."

She picked at the dish in front of her. "Which one is this?"

• • • •

A dutiful wife sat through a bloody western video with her husband, and despite her disdain, she did an admirable job of feigning sincere interest. When it was over, she remarked, "That was a great film."

"Yes! Can we watch it again tomorrow night?"

• • • •

Two guests were observing the honorees at a golden wedding anniversary. "Fifty years of marriage," remarked one. "That's something indeed, for a woman who claims to be 59 years old."

The imminent groom at a wedding rehearsal banquet rose to address his betrothed and their guests. "I have a confession to make to you," he stated to the bride-to-be. "Before I met you, I spent many happy years in the arms of another woman." All in the audience held their breath, aghast. His fiancé went pale. "My mother!" he finished, raising his glass to toast the relieved matron.

Everyone laughed, and one elderly gentleman present made a mental note of the joke for future reference. A few months later, this gentleman was celebrating his golden wedding anniversary at a similar banquet. He rose, glass in hand.

"My dear," he said to his bride of 50 years, "I have a confession to make to you after all these years."

The room fell silent.

"Before I met and fell in love with you, all those generations ago, there was another woman in whose arms I spent many a happy moment. . . "

And he forgot how the joke ended!

• • • •

"My wife and I have it all worked out," said Chester. "I make all the major decisions, she makes all the minor decisions, and we get along beautifully."

"What kinds of minor decisions does she make?" asked his friend Wes.

"Oh, when it's time to buy a new car, for example. Or where young Chester is going to college. Or whether we should move to another town."

"Those are minor? Wow! What kinds of major decisions do you get to make?"

"Practically all the important stuff. Like, who should be the next president, what level of trade should be established with the Ukraine. . . ."

In bygone days, prospectors, pioneers, and farmers in the western territories used to acquire mail-order brides from the East. One such newlywed couple mounted the settler's wagon and drove away toward the farm.

A mile or so out of town, the horse became interested in a roadside haystack and paused for a mouthful. The driver popped his whip and remarked, "That's one."

A few miles farther, the horse was surprised by a fox darting across the rutted road. The horse rose on its hind legs, almost shaking the startled bride off the wagon seat.

"That's two," said the settler, cracking the whip again.

Later, a filly grazing in a distant pasture caught the animal's attention, and the horse drifted out of the ruts.

"That's three," the husband said. He got down from his seat and shot the horse dead without another word.

Incredulous, his bride cried, "Why'd you kill a good horse over a trifle like that?"

The settler gave her a stern look and said, "That's one."

• • • •

"Aren't you ready yet, dear?" an impatient husband asked his wife.

"In a minute!" his wife shouted in exasperation. "I've told you 50 times already."

• • • •

Walt: "I just don't know what to get my wife for our anniversary."
John: "Why don't you ask her what she wants?"
Walt: "Oh, no! That would cost too much."

# LAW & ORDER

A detective was interviewing a witness in the aftermath of a murder. "Are you related to the defendant?"

"Yes. He's my son," the witness acknowledged.

"And was he your son three weeks ago, when this incident occurred?"

• • • •

A lawyer was reading the will of a wealthy deceased client to the assembled beneficiaries. ". . .And I always promised to mention my lazy nephew Larry in my will. Hi, there, Larry. . . ."

• • • •

Lawyer in court: "You testify that the deceased was alive and actually kissed you good-night on the evening of March the 30th?"

Witness: "Yes."

Lawyer: "So he was alive in your neighborhood on the night of the 30th, and on the morning of the 31st he apparently woke up dead at his home?"

• • • •

Trial lawyer, questioning a witness: "Which one got killed—you or your friend?"

• • • •

Lawyer to witness: "Mr. Roper, how did your first marriage end?"

Witness: "It ended in death."

Lawyer: "The death of your spouse?"

Another lawyer, posing a similarly inane question to a witness, caught himself in the middle of it, broke off and besought the judge, "Your honor, I would like to withdraw the next question."

• • • •

Prosecutor: "How far away from the scene of the crime were you when you heard the first shot?"
Witness: "About 30 feet."
Prosecutor: "How far away were you when the second shot was fired?"
Witness: "About 200 yards."

• • • •

Two well-heeled ladies flying first-class condescended, after an hour of silent boredom, to strike up a conversation with each other.

"I just had a delightful note from my son the surgeon," intoned one. "Do you have children?"

"My only son lives in New York."

"And what does he do?"

"He, too, has chosen to pursue the medical profession."

"Lovely. I suppose he's a GP."

"He's a malpractice lawyer."

• • • •

"I've sat at this bench for 12 years," the judge said, "and this is the fifth time you've been brought before me on disorderly conduct charges. Aren't you ashamed?"

The defendant muttered to her lawyer, "He can't get a promotion, and he takes it out on us."

A lawyer was examining a witness in court. "Could you see the defendant's head from where you were seated when the shooting occurred?" the lawyer asked.

"Yes, quite clearly."

"Where did you see it, exactly?"

"It was resting on her shoulders."

• • • •

Patrol Officer: "Why did you drive into the ditch?"

Driver: "I was trying to turn off the blinker."

• • • •

"Did you know the deceased?" asked a lawyer at trial.

"Yes," answered the witness.

"And did you meet the deceased before or after her death?"

• • • •

A judge admonished a defendant, "Are you aware how close this came to being a murder trial and not an attempted murder trial?"

"I believe so, Your Honor. The primary difference, as I see it, is that the rotten scoundrel lived."

• • • •

A defense lawyer left little doubt what he thought of an investigating officer when he posed this question in court: "Have you ever investigated a murder in which there was a victim?"

A rookie on patrol with a veteran cop asked, "What's the fastest way to disperse a mob, without resorting to force?"

"Pass a hat," said the vet.

"Why didn't you report this robbery when you arrived home at mid-morning?" the investigating officer asked the housewife.

"I wasn't sure it was a robbery. I thought at first my husband had simply been looking for his neckties."

• • • •

Lawyer to expert witness: "Dr. Quincy, how many autopsies have you performed on dead people?"

Witness: "All of my autopsies."

• • • •

A sergeant was selecting new police dogs from the training kennels. Most of the animals were excellent, well-disciplined German shepherds, but he noticed one scrawny mixed breed in a separate unit.

"You call that a police dog?" he asked the trainer.

"The absolute best! He's our undercover hound."

• • • •

A lawyer presented a photograph to a defendant on the witness stand. "Is that you, third from the left?"

"Yes, that's me," acknowledged the defendant.

The lawyer then perceived a need to make the record perfectly clear: "Were you present when the picture was taken?"

• • • •

Judge: "How do you plead?"

Defendant: "What's the evidence?"

# MILITARY

The eyes of three generals were scrutinizing the parade grounds when one platoon under the command of a green lieutenant passed before them in review. He managed to order his men correctly through a flashy maneuver, but it left him drained of his composure. To his horror, he found they had completed the procedure by marching straight toward the edge of a lake. Murmurs welled up through the audience as onward the platoon marched. The lieutenant's lips were parched, his throat soundless.

As they approached within 30 feet of the water's edge, his sergeant could stand it no longer and sang out, "Well, Sir, shouldn't we wish them bon voyage?"

• • • •

When Philip of Macedon was conquering Greece, he encountered only one stronghold of real resistance: the city of Sparta. Hoping to convince the Spartans to surrender without the loss of more soldiers, he sent a messenger warning of all the ravages that would come if Philip's army had to take the city by force.

Sparta's reply was one word in length: "If."

Impressed by their confidence, Philip left the city alone.

• • • •

The new Army recruits were rousted out of their bunks at 3:30 a.m. "You're wasting the best part of the day already!" screamed the sergeant.

One recruit turned to another and muttered, "It sure doesn't take long to spend the night around here."

A sailor was smoking on deck one night when he heard footsteps approach. "Gotta light, son?"

"Maybe, but it'll cost you a cigarette."

"You gotta deal."

The sailor casually lit a match and held it to the other's lips. In the flickering light he was horrified to see that the man was not only an officer, but an admiral.

"I beg your pardon, sir," the seaman stammered, snapping to a salute.

"Don't worry," the admiral said. "But you're lucky I'm not a lieutenant j.g."

• • • •

Half a dozen generals sat at the head table at a banquet, and the topic of conversation turned to a recent battle in which their army had been victorious after days of maneuvering, fighting and counter-maneuvering. The dialogue became heated as they debated which of them should get over-all credit for the victory. But the senior general said nothing, until finally they all turned to him for his deadlock-breaking opinion.

"I'm really not sure which of you deserves the credit for winning," he said. "But it's certain that had we lost, I would have received all the credit for that."

• • • •

The trusted old Army mule was laid to rest lovingly by the troops he'd served. Read his epitaph: "HERE LIES GEORGIE, WHO KICKED TWO COLONELS, TWO CAPTAINS, FOUR LIEUTENANTS, THREE SERGEANTS, A CORPORAL, SIX PRIVATES, AND ONE LAND MINE."

A buck private was on guard duty one night when a major approached. Without saluting, the private merely nodded and continued marching to and fro.

The major was incensed. "I am a major," he shouted, "and you, son, are in deep trouble!"

"Not as deep as you," the private replied. "The sergeant's been searching the whole post for you for the last three hours."

# OPTOMETRISTS

An optometrist examining an elderly patient asked, "Can you read the fifth line on the chart?"

"No."

"How about the fourth line?"

"No."

"Hmm. Try the second line."

"I can't read that one, either."

"Surely you can read the first line."

"Truth is, I've never learned to read."

• • • •

An American optometrist examined a Japanese national and reported bluntly, "You have a cataract."

"No, no," the patient corrected. "I drive a Rincoln Continentar."

• • • •

"Bad news, Mrs. Brown," her eye doctor said. "I'm afraid it's time for you to wear glasses."

"I'm afraid it's time for you to wear glasses," she retorted. "I have mine on."

Eye Doctor: "Please read the fourth line of the chart hanging on the door."
Patient: "Door? What door?"

# OTHER DRIVERS

What goes "VROOM! SCREECH! VROOM! SCREECH! VROOM!"

A student driver negotiating a caution blinker.

• • • •

The minister's wife was a bundle of nerves riding with her husband. She'd long since given up playing the role of driving instructor and was reduced to cowering in the passenger seat, biting her fingernails.

"Don't worry," her husband intoned, sliding around a corner, rushing belatedly to an evening service at a crosstown church. "The Lord is riding with us."

"You'd better slow down," she responded weakly. "You're liable to kill Him any moment."

• • • •

"Why did you run that red light?" a highway patrol officer demanded, approaching the driver of a car he'd pulled over.

"I think my car is color-blind."

• • • •

"Why do you have 'VT-336' tattooed across your rump?" asked the doctor, examining a patient.

"That's no tattoo," said the patient. "That's where my wife backed into me with the car."

A man lay in the middle of the street, his ear to the pavement. A passer-by stopped, leaned close and listened as the man reported, "Red Chevy, wire wheels, young driver. Two-door, I think. Montana plates, T3R-777."

The passer-by was impressed. "You can tell that just by listening to the pavement?"

"That's a description of the car that just ran me down."

• • • •

Hal: "Why do you keep a coat hanger in your car?"
Bob: "In case I lock my keys inside."

• • • •

"I was driving well under the speed limit, minding my own business," testified the traffic court defendant. "Suddenly another driver appeared in my lane and smashed into my car."

"And what was the other person driving?" asked the prosecutor.

"A tree."

• • • •

A farmer was driving his expectant wife to the hospital for delivery.

"Do you think we're getting close to the city?" she moaned.

"I expect so. I'm having to dodge an awful lot of pedestrians."

• • • •

A couple was driving through the rain when their car began to hydroplane. The husband's hands gripped the wheel, his knuckles white. "I can't control it!" he exclaimed.

"Well, try to hit something inexpensive!" his wife advised.

A woman was maneuvering in her car along a mountain road. Rounding one sharp bend, she met a man driving the other way. He stuck his head out the window and yelled at her, "Cow!"

Incensed, she yelled back, "Imbecile!"

Rounding the next turn, she slammed on brakes to avoid a cow clomping mindlessly along the middle of the road.

• • • •

Two cars arrived perpendicularly at a four-way stop about the same moment. One driver figured she'd missed the advantage by a split second, so she waited for the other driver to make a move. . .and waited. . .and waited.

Finally, it became obvious to her that the other driver was waiting for her to make the first move. So she eased into the crossing—and instantly was struck broadside by the other vehicle.

Blessedly, it was only a fender bender. But the other driver stormed out the door and framed herself angrily in the window. "What gave you the right," the other woman demanded, "to assume I'd finished making up my mind?"

• • • •

A man was daydreaming at a traffic light. It changed to green. . .then yellow and red again. Still he sat, his mind a million miles away.

The driver behind him eased her car around to the side, rolled down her window and asked, "What color are you waiting for?"

Nick: "They say that in downtown Atlanta someone is run down every day, on the average."
Vick: "Well, why don't they get that poor soul off the streets?"

• • • •

Two business colleagues on Monday morning set off along the interstate at about 20 miles over the speed limit. The driver, oblivious to the speedometer, was ebullient. "I love the first day of the week," he said. "Bright sun rising, clear blue sky, not much traffic. Don't you find it thrilling to be alive?"

"Thrilling?" his partner muttered nervously. "I think it's absolutely unbelievable."

• • • •

A woman's car was stalled at a four-way stop, and try as she might, she couldn't coax it to start. Confusion in every direction was the result, and cars were backed up. The man driving the car directly behind hers honked his horn mercilessly, and other drivers joined the cacophony.

At length the woman got out of her car and walked back to the haranguer. "Would you care to exchange places?" she asked innocently. "You go up there and try to start my car, and I'll stay back here and blow your horn at you."

• • • •

A patrol officer stopped an elderly gentleman in his car. "You turned left without signaling and almost caused a wreck," the officer said.

"Why should I have to signal?" the driver asked indignantly. "This is where I always turn to go home."

A passerby saw a car run off the road, hit a tree and start to burn. Stopping, the observer ran to the wrecked car, opened the door, dragged the driver to a safe distance and gently laid him on the grass. "Are you comfortable?" the Samaritan asked.

"Oh, we're not what you'd call rich," mumbled the victim, "but we get by."

# PARACHUTES

A skydiving student apprehensively made his first jump. True to his worst fears, the parachute failed to open. Happily, he had the presence of mind to pull the ripcord of the safety chute—but it, too, failed to open.

Terrified, he was amazed to see a man, arms flailing, rising from the earth like a rocket to meet him. The man's ascent leveled off just as they met, and they fell together.

"Do. . .do. . .do you know anything about parachutes?" the student ventured.

"Afraid n-not. Do you know anything about h-hot water heaters?"

• • • •

An Army trainee jumped out of the troop plane and pulled the ripcord of his parachute. Nothing happened. He pulled the emergency chute's ripcord. Still no result.

But the fellow was an optimist. "Well," he said to himself as the ground approached, "so far, so good."

Aboard the plane for the first practice jump, one nervous Ranger trainee couldn't suppress his apprehension. "Suppose the parachute doesn't open," he asked the sergeant.

"Just return it to the commissary. They'll give you a new one."

# PERSPECTIVE

"There's Mr. Worthington. He's such a cheerful man. Even when things go wrong, he's always smiling."

"That's because he has people to blame them on."

• • • •

A ranch hand had the rare honor of being invited inside the big ranch house for Thanksgiving dinner. Dressed in his best, he still appeared quite crude compared to most of the guests. But he seemed uninhibited about being rawly conspicuous.

"The bathroom is just down the hall," said the pretty rancher's daughter. "You may wash up for dinner in there."

"Oh, that's all right, Ma'am," he replied. "I warshed first thing this mornin' out at the water trough."

• • • •

Two women were facing each other in the waiting room at a bus station. One said to the other, "I'm sorry, but I'm a little hard of hearing. Could you speak up?"

The other replied, "I haven't said anything. I'm chewing gum."

A family on vacation were driving through rolling farmland. "See that herd of cows?" Mother pointed out. "How many do you suppose there are, children?"

"A hundred and four," Melody answered immediately.

"How did you count them so fast?" her brother asked.

"I didn't, actually. I counted the 416 legs and divided by four."

. . . .

"What do you think of Shakespeare?" one student asked another.

The other shrugged. "All of his writing is really just a collection of well-known quotations thrown together into somewhat cohesive plots."

. . . .

"I can prescribe a hearing aid that will improve your hearing by 30 percent," the doctor told Mr. Zane, an octogenarian. "But it'll cost you more than a thousand dollars."

"I'll keep my money, and you may keep your device," Mr. Zane said. "I'm 86 years old. Reckon I've heard enough already."

. . . .

A business tycoon fell on hard times and was reported to have shrugged it away with a smile. "Bad luck," he said.

A few years later he was back on his feet and had become one of the wealthiest men within a four-state radius. He was asked if "luck" was behind the abrupt upturn. "Luck," he proclaimed, "had nothing at all to do with it."

A rich man and a poor man were arguing about which was happiest.

"My millions make me extremely happy," said the rich man. "Money assures me of excellent housing, fine cars, the best food, vacations whenever and wherever I want, the best possible medical treatment and total security. All you have to show are six children and a lot of debt."

"But I'm more contented than you," countered the poor man. "If I had your money, I'd want more. If you had six children, you wouldn't want anymore."

• • • •

A young man was boarding an airplane for his first flight. He was very bashful, and found to his dismay that he'd been assigned a center seat between two attractive young ladies.

Settling in with far more discomfort than normally attends airline travel in a center seat, he wondered what to say or how to act. The words of a dear old uncle happily came to him: "Whenever you're around women you don't know, just ask them if they're married and if they have any children, and they'll do all the talking after that."

He braced himself and turned to the woman on his left. "Do you have any children?"

"Why, yes!" she answered eagerly. "A gorgeous little girl named Heather."

"Are you married?" he continued.

Her friendliness instantly became ice, and she returned to the magazine she'd been reading.

"Must've asked the questions in the wrong order," he thought to himself.

He turned to the woman on his right. "Are you married?" he asked.

"Well. . .no," she responded suspiciously.

"Do you have any children?"

Lost in an unfamiliar neighborhood, a man stopped and asked directions to a house. The woman rocking on the porch seemed to know exactly where to direct him.

"Go back up the road from where you came, two-and-a-quarter miles. Turn at the video store on South Lake Drive. On the fourth block you'll go around an S curve and you'll see it—a big, blue, two-story house with black trim, a gazebo and a goldfish pond."

"Is it on the right or left?"

"Oh, I'm not good at details like that."

• • • •

A reporter asked an aging statesman what he would like for people to say about him 50 years from now. "He looks young for his age," replied the statesman.

• • • •

A little girl sat down at a library table next to three men who were having an apparent argument over the spelling of the word "room."

"I'd spell it 'rrrom,' " one man said.

"Nah, that's not the way it sounds at all," scoffed another. " 'It's roommm.' "

"No way," said the third. "Two 'r's, two 'o's and two 'm's, plain and simple."

The little girl picked up her book in disgust and rose to leave. "It's spelled 'r-o-o-m,' " she informed them, and walked away to find a seat where the conversation was more intelligent.

The men looked at each other. "I don't think I can take her word for it," said one. "I seriously doubt she's ever been on the flight deck of an aircraft carrier when those jets are taking off."

Larry was considered a simpleton by the people in his town, and they often made fun of him.

"There's old Larry. Watch this," said one college youth, showing a visiting pal around the village.

The host took a nickel and a dime from his pocket and held them out to Larry. "One's for you, Larry," he said. "Take your pick."

Larry immediately pocketed the nickel.

"See?" the teaser said. "He thinks a nickel is worth more than a dime because it's larger."

Later in the weekend, the visitor was wandering the streets alone when he encountered Larry. He felt sorry for the lad and determined to set the record straight.

"Tell me something, Larry," he said. "You realize a dime is worth more than a nickel, don't you?"

"Sure," Larry said.

"Then why do you take a nickel instead of a dime when someone offers you a choice?"

"As long as they think I don't know what I'm doing, I maintain a steady income that way."

• • • •

A teen-ager asked his lifeguard friend, "What's the best way to teach a girl to swim?"

His buddy thought a moment. "Is she your sister or your girlfriend?"

"My sister."

"Well, I'd suggest the old-fashioned way. Push her into the pool and tell her she's got a choice: Sink or swim."

A woman went around her neighborhood selling club raffle tickets. The next week, she happened to meet one of the neighbors, who asked who'd won the grand prize.

"Believe it or not," she said, embarrassed, "my little girl won. Isn't that something?"

"Yes," said the neighbor with a smile. "Who won second prize?"

"I feel strange admitting it, but my husband had the winning ticket."

"And the third prize?" asked the neighbor, still smiling.

"You know, I won that myself. It was an incredibly lucky week for my family." She looked thoughtfully at the neighbor. "By the way, I don't believe you've paid me yet for your tickets."

"No," said the smiling neighbor. "Lucky week for me, too."

# PSYCHIATRISTS

"What's your problem?" asked the psychiatrist.

"It may not be a problem, but I think I'm a horse."

"Yep, that's definitely a problem. It'll take time to cure you—and it won't be cheap."

"I'm not too worried about the money. I've won the Kentucky Derby already."

• • • •

Psychiatrist: "What seems to be your problem?"
Patient: "I can't make up my mind about anything."
Psychiatrist: "Is this a recent phenomenon?"
Patient: "Yes. . .and no."

A patient barged in on her psychiatrist and screamed, "I think I'm a cat!"

The psychiatrist gently consoled her. "Just sit down, and we'll discuss this."

"You know I'm not allowed on the furniture. . . ."

• • • •

An agitated patient was stomping around the psychiatrist's office, running his hands through his hair, almost in tears. "Doctor, my memory's gone. Gone! I can't remember my wife's name. Can't remember my children's names. Can't remember what kind of car I drive. Can't remember where I work. It was all I could do to find my way here."

"Calm down. How long have you been like this?"

"Like what?"

• • • •

"Tell me why you hate your father," a psychiatrist prompted his patient.

"Hate my father? Why, I don't. My father is a wonderful man."

"Listen," the psychiatrist said. "You have to cooperate with us if you want to be cured."

• • • •

A woman was sharing with a friend her husband's state of mind. "Walter's psychiatrist has done him a world of good. He used to refuse to answer the phone when it rang. Now he answers it even when is doesn't ring."

"You are far too preoccupied with material things," pronounced a psychiatrist at the conclusion of a long session with a new patient. "Money, a prestigious home, fine clothes, luxury car, vacation house, yacht—you're driving yourself crazy, working unbelievable hours, acquiring these things. Think about it. These symbols are really expendable in your life. Money means absolutely nothing, in the end. You should learn to do without, and you would be so much happier.

"Now, let's see. Forty minutes. . .That will come to $800."

• • • •

A man barged into a psychiatrist's office and demanded, "You've got to help me. Everybody's ignoring me. Is it just my imagination?"

The psychiatrist called to the receptionist, "Would you send in the next patient, please?"

• • • •

"My little Wally thinks he's an astronaut," a woman complained to a psychiatrist on the phone. "He's constantly walking around in slow motion, pretending he's weightless. And he calls out scientific-sounding orders to nobody in particularly. He's living in a daze."

"It's quite understandable. He's been profoundly influenced by movies like *Star Trek, Apollo 13*. He'll soon grow out of it—but in the long run, it actually could turn out to be a good influence."

"That's wonderful! I'll go tell his wife!"

"I spend hours every day in front of a mirror admiring my beauty," a woman said to her psychiatrist. "Does that necessarily indicate I have a problem with vanity?"

"Could be that, or perhaps a bizarre imagination."

# REGIONAL HUMOR

In northern Minnesota it's so cold some people sleep between the mattresses.

• • • •

Teacher: "What can you tell us about the climate in Greenland?"
Student: "It's so cold there that the inhabitants have to live in other countries."

• • • •

Two mountaineers were discussing foreign countries. "I hear tell that in Israel the weather stays about the same all year round," one commented.

"That be so?" said the other, disturbed. "What in the world do they ever talk about, then?"

• • • •

A woman stepped up to the agent's window at a small-town bus station. "Would you please tell me what time it is?" she asked. "I have to catch a bus to Dayton."

"Today's Thursday," the agent said.

"I know what day it is. I want to know the time. And what time is the next bus to Dayton, please?"

"Today's Thursday," the agent repeated. "Next bus to Dayton won't be through here till next Monday afternoon."

In northern Maine they say there are two seasons:
"winter" and "roadwork."

• • • •

A tourist speeding through isolated mountain towns stopped
at a ramshackle store for a soda. "By the way," he asked the
proprietor, "what's the speed limit in these parts?"

"You can go as fast as you want to," was the answer. "As
a matter of fact, I don't think you can get out of here fast
enough to suit us."

• • • •

A Minnesota farm family was driving home from their
Lutheran church one Sunday, and the smallest boy was in a
foul frame of mind. "Why is it," he mumbled, "that our
pastor talks about St. Paul all the time and never mentions
Minneapolis?"

# SCHOOL DAYS

Teacher: "Why was it said that in Victorian England, the
sun never set on the British Empire?"
Student: "Because the sun sets in the west, and England is
in the east."

• • • •

English teacher: "You lost 10 points on your test for mis-
spelling, Cindy. You need to remember: It's 'i' before 'e'
except after 'c.' "
Cindy: "Did anybody ever explain that to Einstein?"

"What are the main parts of the human eye?" asked the science teacher.

Little Susan still had her mind on the Sunday school lesson of the day before. "The pupil, mote and beam," she answered.

• • • •

"Dad, I'm sleepy. Will you do my homework for me?"

"You know I can't do that. It would be wrong."

"I don't care, as long as you give it your best effort."

• • • •

"Mom, I've learned to write!" little Scott shouted, coming home from his first day at school.

"Wonderful!" said his mother. "What can you write?"

Scott scratched his head. "I'm not sure. They haven't taught us to read yet."

• • • •

The first grade teacher on the opening day of school asked a student if he knew how to count.

"Yes," he beamed. "I learned from Daddy."

"Let me hear you count from 5 to 10."

The child did as he was asked.

"Now, do you know what comes after 10?"

"Jack!"

• • • •

History Teacher: "Michael, who was President Eisenhower's opponent in the 1956 election?"

Michael: "I don't remember—in fact, I don't think I was born yet."

Teacher: "Michelle, construct a sentence using the word 'dour.' "

Michelle, after thinking a while: "May I use an example from a hymn?"

Teacher: "I suppose so."

Michelle: " 'O God, dour help in ages past. . . .' "

• • • •

"What was the most depressing time of your life?"

"Probably the three years I spent in second grade."

• • • •

Little Winston came home from school dejected.

"What's wrong?" asked his mother.

"Claustrophobia."

"Claustrophobia? I didn't know you were afraid of enclosed places."

"I'm not. I missed that word on my spelling test."

• • • •

Two boys were entering the classroom on exam day. "I don't care if it is unconstitutional," said one. "I'm saying a prayer before this one."

• • • •

Teacher 1: "I don't know what to do with Jack. He's in fourth grade and he can barely count past 10."

Teacher 2: "I don't think he's worried. His life's ambition is to be a boxing referee."

• • • •

Three magic words for school teachers:
June, July and August.

A school principal called a child's parents into conference. "It's about your daughter," the principal said.

"Is she cheating?" the mother asked, distressed.

"Oh, no way. Not with grades like hers."

• • • •

A teacher asked his high school seniors to express in writing the most valuable thing they believed they would take with them after twelve years of study. He was not at all encouraged by the response of one scholar: "I am real greatfull to all the teachers who hav contribut to my exsullent edumacation."

• • • •

Teacher 1: "I really like Cindy, but she's a terrible student. Almost everything she writes on her test papers is inaccurate."

Teacher 2: "It's okay. She plans to be a weather forecaster when she grows up."

• • • •

A teacher approached young Horace shaking her head. "Your handwriting is absolutely unreadable," she said. "You're bound for failure in life, if no one can read what you write. The only option I see is for you to become a doctor."

• • • •

An English teacher kept this wood-carved sign above her classroom door: DEPARTMENT OF REDUNDANCY DEPARTMENT.

A senior class had behaved abominably at an assembly program, and at the end the school principal announced sternly that there would be no outdoor recess for them for the remainder of the week.

As he turned from the podium, from the middle of the crowded assembly hall came a shout: "Give me liberty, or give me death!"

"Who said that?" demanded the principal, wheeling about.

There was a short silence. Then another anonymous voice called out, "Patrick Henry?"

•  •  •  •

A history teacher was giving a verbal quiz. The focus was on the year 1912.

"What famous disaster occurred that year?" she asked.

Martin, the brash whiz kid of the class, predictably beat everyone to the answer. "The Titanic struck an iceberg!"

"Yes," said the teacher. "And where did it occur?"

"North Atlantic!" It was Martin again.

"What month?" pressed the teacher.

"April!" Martin piped up. "12th of April!"

The teacher was becoming impatient with Martin's quick answers at the expense of everyone else.

"How many passengers and crew perished?" she pressed.

"1,517!"

Martin was beaming, indomitable—until she turned squarely to face him with her last question: "And their names?"

Fourth-grade teacher: "Cheryl, what state do you think you would like to live in above all the others?"

Cheryl: "Massachusetts. That's where they had the Boston Tea Party and the first battles of the American Revolution."

Teacher: "That's very good! And how do you spell Massachusetts?"

Cheryl: "Mas. . . . Now that I think of it, I'd rather live in New York."

• • • •

A mother was signing her daughter's report card, as required. The father, watching across the table, asked, "You're signing your name with an 'X?' "

"Yes. With grades like that, I don't want her teacher to think she comes from a literate family."

• • • •

Mother: "Why don't you like school?"
Son: "Oh, it's just the principal of the thing."

• • • •

Teacher: "What is the deepest part of the Indian Ocean?"
Student: "The bottom."

# SCIENCE

The library lecture series for the week was on the topic "Dietary Maintenance of the Liver and Kidneys."

"Wonderful," commented one attendee, browsing the hand-out materials. "I love organ recitals."

NASA scientists have an ingenious way of determining whether a distant planet is inhabited. They program the landing craft to mechanically dig a hole in the surface. If no one comes to stand around and watch, they know the planet is void of life.

. . . .

The family was very proud when John graduated from college, for every member of their previous generations was illiterate. A sumptuous feast was prepared in his honor, with many friends and neighbors gathered around the farmhouse for the occasion.

John was a physics major. "Now tell us about physics," beamed his father, as the family and friends lounged around the front porch after the meal.

The son was caught off-guard. He stammered, "Physics is about. . .it involves. . . . Haven't you heard of Albert Einstein?"

"Yes, I believe I recall the name."

"Well, he was the world's foremost physicist."

"What did he do?"

"Why, he came up with the theory of relativity."

Blank stares stabbed John from every direction. As he endeavored to explain the concept of relativity, the stares turned to head shakes and murmurs.

The father was as baffled as everyone else. "I reckon all that must have been fun for old Einstein," he allowed. "But what did he do for a living?"

The biology teacher placed several small baggies on the podium and announced, "Today we will be dissecting frogs. These are fresh specimens my husband collected for us yesterday evening."

She opened each bag and distributed it to a small group of students to take back to the wash basins. The fourth bag she opened, however, contained not a frog, but a slice of quiche.

The teacher's hand went to her mouth. "What on earth," she gasped, "did I have for lunch?"

# SOUP & SALAD

"Waitress, this plate is wet."
"Of course. That's your soup."

• • • •

"Waiter, there's a fly in my soup."
"Yes, I think it's the humidity that kills them."

• • • •

"Waitress, there's a fly in my soup."
"I'm terribly sorry, Madame. I know you find that terribly offensive."
"Not really. It's just that I prefer to dine alone."

• • • •

"Waitress, there's a fly in my soup."
"For $2.95, what did you expect? Duck?"

"This salad actually has dirt in it," complained Farmer Sikes.

"I'm sorry," said Mrs. Sikes. "I must not have washed the lettuce leaves quite clean. At least it's a happy reminder we're eating fresh vegetables!"

"Vegetables are something we're supposed to eat," grumbled her husband. "Soil is something we're supposed to plow."

•  •  •  •

"Waiter, there's a fly in my soup. What's the meaning of this?"

"I'm just a server, not a philosopher."

•  •  •  •

"Waitress, there's a dead fly in my soup."

"Oh, no! It was alive in the kitchen."

•  •  •  •

"Waiter, there's something alive in my soup. What is it?"

"Hmm. Not sure. The bugs around here all look alike to me."

•  •  •  •

"Waiter, there's a fly in my soup."

"Not so loud—the other guests might want one."

•  •  •  •

Diner: "What's this bowl of stuff?"

Waitress: "That's bean soup."

Diner: "I didn't ask what it's been. What is it at the moment?"

# SPORTS

"How'd you bruise your shins?" asked Pete. "Rugby?"

"Naw," Jack said. "My wife talked me into being her bridge partner."

• • • •

The quarterback went down and a penalty flag went flying onto the pile-up.

"Whasa matter?" demanded a bulky defensive end, rising to his feet and towering above the official.

"Late hit," said the ref.

"So? I couldn't get here any faster."

• • • •

A golfer lounging in the pro shop remarked to a friend, "I've always suspected Greg of cheating on his scorecard. Today I obtained conclusive proof."

"How?"

"I was with him when he hit a hole in one. Afterward, I noticed he recorded it as a zero."

• • • •

"My son is on the football team this year," said Mrs. Lowell.

"Splendid," said Mrs. Packard. "What position does he play?"

"I think he plays drawback."

A tribal chieftain returned to his native country after a visit to the United States. "The Americans," he reported to his people, "have greater magic than us."

"Can they make it rain?" asked a tribeswoman.

"Whenever they want."

"How?"

"They gather thousands of people around a flat, green meadow. Warriors blowing horns and beating drums line up at each end of the meadow and make strange music. Then women wearing few clothes and shaking little clumps of grass run between the warriors onto the meadow, pursued by other warriors wearing colorful, shiny headdresses. They do this at both ends of the meadow. Then the two groups of warriors wearing funny headdresses at both ends of the meadow form themselves into lines facing each other. One group of warriors kicks a brown ball to the other group, and they all clash and fight for the ball.

"And then it begins to rain."

• • • •

The high school football coach was having a word with the general math teacher. With a bit of leniency, he suggested, the teacher could give the star fullback a passing grade and let him remain on the team.

The math teacher shook his head and presented the coach with the fullback's latest test paper. "Look at this. He thinks 10 times 12 is 150. He put 16 times 4 equals 435."

The coach fumed in exasperation. "You gotta be such a perfectionist?"

• • • •

Who was the first championship tennis player?
Sir Gallahad. He won the Grail Cup.

A duffer lounging at the clubhouse was telling friends about his upcoming vacation adventure to the Australian Outback. "I'll be alone, hundreds of miles from civilization," he said with a salty blend of anxiety and haughtiness.

"Take these along." The club pro offered a bag of old, well-used clubs.

"To the Outback? What in the world for?"

"In case you get lost."

"And what am I supposed to do? 'Drive' my way out?"

"Nope. Just drop a ball on the ground and start plundering through the bag, and at least three guys will appear out of nowhere and tell you which iron to use."

• • • •

It was sportscaster Howard Cossell who defined sports as "the toy department of human life."

• • • •

Tal had invested a lot of money on SCUBA equipment and training. Finally the day came when he felt confident going down alone.

He had descended on an offshore wreck about 50 feet below the surface when he saw a guy approach with no diving gear at all, not even a snorkel. The guy groped around for a minute or two and seemed in no hurry to go topside for air.

Miffed, Tal got out his message slate and wrote, "How do you do this with no breathing apparatus?"

The visitor scrawled in return, "I'm drowning!"

The club pro was obligated to play a round of golf with each new member, though he often found it painfully tedious. Such was the case with McClaren, a newcomer to town who, word had it, was a dismal duffer.

McClaren arrived for their game nattily dressed, sporting the finest clubs the pro had ever seen. The pro had expected as much—the worst players typically flash the most expensive equipment. Imagine the pro's shock when, on the first hole, McClaren hit a beautiful drive that bounced onto the green, made a beeline for the flag and rolled neatly into the cup for a hole in one!

Imagine his double surprise when, on the second hole, the "duffer" repeated the feat.

On the third hole, it appeared McClaren's opening drive would yield still a third miracle. The ball hopped onto the green, curved sharply to conform perfectly to the slope of the grass, arched beautifully toward the cup . . .and came to rest two inches short.

McClaren turned to the pro and shrugged his shoulders. "What could I expect?" he said sadly. "This is only the third time I've played the stupid game."

• • • •

"What was the score of the football game?"

"We beat them 38-0—and they were lucky to score that much."

• • • •

"Well, at least our boys are good losers," the proud football father said after his son's team had lost its fifth consecutive game.

"I'd say they're just about perfect losers," whispered the mother.

A junior business associate was asked to play a round of golf with the boss. He was understandably nervous, because he was an extremely good golfer, and he knew his boss to be extremely poor.

The junior played a very conservative game, hoping to keep the score at least close. Unfortunately, he forgot his professional relations strategy and hit one beautiful tee shot that spanned the length of the fairway, bounced onto the green and rolled within a couple of feet of the cup. Compounding the felony, he inadvertently put his hand to his mouth and uttered, "Oops!"

• • • •

Miss Winkler had never seen a football game, her own interest leaning decidely toward the arts. After her first gridiron experience, she described to a friend what she had seen:

"It's quite atrocious. They organize themselves into two opposing lines. One team kicks the ball to the other team, then chases the ball, and they get into a fight."

She shook her head in disgust. "If they want it so badly, they should never kick it away to begin with."

• • • •

A golfer noticed her partner was using a peculiar ball. It had several threadlike, quarter-inch antennae bobbing from its surface.

"What kind of ball is that?"

"It's a security ball," said her partner. "I can't possibly lose it. No matter where it ends up, I can always home into it electronically."

"I've never heard of those. Where can you buy them?"

"Actually, I found it in the rough beside the eighth fairway last week."

A father was angered by his child's unmitigated swearing on the little league football field.

"Do you know what happens to youngsters who talk like that?" he asked, taking his boy aside.

"Yeah. They grow up to be pros."

# TELEPHONES

A child was doing his homework and asked, "Mommy, was it Thomas Edison who invented the talking machine?"

"No," his mother answered. "God invented the talking machine. Edison invented a way to turn it off."

• • • •

Fran: "Got a call from a telemarketing scam artist last night."
John: "What makes you so sure it was a scam?"
Fran: "She was soliciting contributions for the widow of the Unknown Soldier."

• • • •

The phone rings. "Hello."
"Is this 555-5555?"
"Yes, it is."
"Would you mind calling 911 for me? My finger's stuck in the dial."

TVs and power speakers were creating a chaotic audio backdrop in the store's home entertainment department. "I really don't know why I'm shopping here," a woman shouted to the clerk above the noise. "I'm buying a birthday gift for my husband, and what he really needs is some peace and quiet."

"We have just the thing!" offered the clerk. She rounded an aisle and returned momentarily with a small package.

"What is it?" asked the wife.

"The ultimate gift for peace and quiet: the phoneless cord."

• • • •

A woman was trying to get a number for a long-distance listing and encountered a less-than-amicable operator.

"You'll have to speak more clearly," the operator snapped. "I can't understand you."

"The name I want is Webster, T.L. Webster."

"You'll have to spell that."

"Webster. 'W' as in 'world'—"

" 'W' as in what?"

# THEOLOGY

A little girl in Sunday school was asked to tell what she'd learned about Esau. "Esau," she defined, "was Jacob's brother who wrote fables and traded his copyright for a bowl of soup."

"Daddy, what did the preacher mean when he said Jesus healed sick people of divers diseases?"

"Oh, don't you worry about that. You don't even swim yet."

• • • •

A young preacher, nervous while conducting his first service, became alarmed halfway through his sermon to notice practically no one was paying attention.

"Can you hear me in the back?" he interrupted his message to call out.

"Not very well," came a distant voice—whereupon everyone in the first 10 rows got up and moved to the back.

• • • •

An angry reader phoned the editor of the local newspaper. "This morning's edition reports me as being dead!" he shrieked.

After a moment of silence, the editor asked, "Where are you calling from?"

• • • •

"That's a lovely picture," the Sunday school teacher told Patricia, "but what is it?"

"God," answered Patricia.

"But dear, we don't know what God looks like."

"Just wait 'til I'm finished, and you'll see."

Two American GIs in World War II were crouched in a foxhole as night fell. One closed his eyes and thanked the Lord out loud for bringing him through another day.

"You know," said his buddy, "a lot of Germans are Christians. They pray to God just like we do. I bet some of 'em are over there prayin' that same prayer right now."

The other GI thought that over a few minutes, then wondered aloud, "Do you really think the Lord understands German?"

• • • •

A church bulletin item announcing a covered dish supper concluded: "Prayer and medication to follow."

• • • •

A pastor was pleasantly surprised at the end of the Sunday service to greet in the reception line a friend whom he knew to be a hardened agnostic.

"It's a pleasure to have you here today!" the pastor said, smiling genuinely. "Might we expect to see you more often?"

"I'm not sure about that," the agnostic said. "I just come once in a while to buy a little life insurance."

• • • •

Jeb: "Did you know the Bible says bigamy is all right?"
Ezra: "No, I reckon the Bible's against bigamy."
Jeb: "But don't you recall all those Old Testament fellers who had lots of wives?"
Ezra: "Yep. But then the Saviour came along and told us no man can serve two masters."

"I think he needs to wear a watch," Mr. Butler said of the new preacher.

"Or at least a calendar," said Mrs. Butler.

• • • •

"When did Adam and Eve eat the apple?" a Sunday school teacher asked.

"In the summertime," answered a student.

"Why Brenda, how do you know that?" the teacher asked.

"Well, we all know it was just before the fall."

• • • •

A young girl walking through a cemetery with her parents was impressed by the eloquent epitaph on every tombstone.

"I wonder," she observed aloud, "where all the terrible people in the world are buried."

• • • •

Mrs. Green: "What do you think of the new preacher?"
Mrs. Gold: "Frankly, he bothers me. He preaches so all-fired long I can't stay awake, but he gets to shoutin' so loud I can't go to sleep."

• • • •

Sunday school teacher: "Peggy, in what order do we find the historical books of the Old Testament?"
Peggy: "They come one right after another."

A mother peeked in to hear her child say his prayers at bedtime. The boy had been in a fussy mood, and his sentences came in mumbled fragments.

"I can't hear what you're saying," his mother gently admonished.

"I'm not praying to you," the child pouted.

• • • •

"Brandy, can you tell us about Good Friday?" the Sunday school teacher asked.

"Sure! That's who helped Robinson Crusoe!"

• • • •

Sunday school teacher: "Tom, did you study your lesson for today?"

Tom: "Yes, Ma'am."

Teacher: "Then tell us all about Job."

Tom: "Job was afflicted on all sides. He lost his livestock, his friends deserted him, he was covered with sores, and he had to go live alone in the desert with his wife."

• • • •

A father listened at the door to his son's bedtime supplications. Suddenly, the child shouted at the top of his lungs, ". . .And for my birthday, please send me a new FOOTBALL HELMET!"

The father stepped inside the door and interrupted. "Not so loud! Your grandmother's trying to sleep in the next room."

"I know. That's why I was hollering about the football helmet."

"We need to have an unscheduled meeting of the board following the morning worship service," the preacher announced. "It should last only a few minutes."

The board members were surprised to be joined at the meeting by a first-time visitor.

"Brother, I'm afraid this meeting is only for the board," the minister advised him.

"I," replied the guest, "am thoroughly bored by your sermons."

• • • •

A mother looked into her child's bedroom to make sure her daughter had performed her nightly details. The little girl drowsily was concluding her prayers with "Amen."

"Did you brush your teeth, dear?" the mother asked.

No answer.

"You know you have to brush your teeth, Donna."

"Aw, Mom, they're clean enough, and I'm sleepy."

A small debate ensued. The mother, hoping for a quick resolution, proclaimed, "You know the Lord wants all of His children to brush their teeth at least three times a day."

"Oh, I don't think so, Mom. I'll ask Him."

Donna buried her head under her pillow. In a moment came a muted but powerful pronouncement: "No! Of course not!"

• • • •

A ship crew was wrecked on a small island, on the verge of starvation. Most gave themselves up to despair, but one began to pray: "Lord, I'm still a young man. There's so much I can do in life if You will just give me a chance. If You'll rescue me, I promise —"

"Hold it, there!" shouted a companion. "Don't commit to anything yet. There's a ship on the horizon."

A minister was explaining the meaning of Pentecost during his children's sermon. "Today we're celebrating a birthday," he said, gesturing to the colorful helium balloons adorning the sanctuary. "It's the birthday of God's church. It's the birthday of all of us here."

He waited a moment for the youngsters to digest the concept. "And after the service, we're all going to the fellowship hall to have a piece of birthday cake!"

To which a small voice inquired, "Is God going to blow out the candles?"

• • • •

Aboard an airplane, Mr. Wilson overheard the flight attendant address his seatmate as "Dr. Adams."

"So, you're a doctor, eh?" Mr. Wilson said. "I've been meaning to ask one of you fellas about a pain I have in my right side."

"I'm afraid I wouldn't be able to help you," the other passenger said pleasantly. "My training is in the area of homiletics."

Mr. Wilson was silent for awhile. Then he asked, "Homiletics—is that fatal?"

• • • •

A clock-watching parishioner couldn't refrain from commenting to the minister after a church service, "Your sermons begin well enough, but why do you make them so long? I'm afraid a lot of folks lose interest."

Replied the minister, "Sermonettes make for Christian-ettes."

Torrential rains were swiftly flooding the town's streets. A preacher sat on his porch watching the deluge. As the rising water approached his front steps, a rescue squad boat motored by. "Come aboard, Preacher!" shouted one of the officials. "We'll carry you to safety."

"I'm safe enough," the preacher replied. "I'm trusting the Lord to protect me and my home."

Half an hour later the water was up to the porch floor. Another boat glided past. "Jump aboard, Preacher! It's going to get worse!"

"I'm not afraid, friends. The Lord will deliver me from drowning."

Late in the day, the flood had almost engulfed the town's buildings. The preacher was on the roof, clinging to the chimney, when a helicopter hovered overhead. A rope was cranked down to the pitiful victim—and astonishingly, the preacher waved the crew away. "The Lord Himself will save me," he declared.

And as darkness descended, the preacher was swept to his death.

The next thing he knew, he was at heaven's gate, waiting at the desk of St. Peter. The venerable saint looked up from his writing. "You!" he exclaimed. "What are you doing here already?"

"Well," the preacher stammered, "I was down there in the flood, waiting for the Lord to rescue me, and finally the water just got too high and. . . ."

"Saints, man! We sent you two boats and a helicopter!"

• • • •

The preacher's small son once was asked by a friend if his father ever preached the same sermon twice.

"Oh, sure. But he never shouts at the same place twice."

A Catholic priest and Jewish rabbi were seated together at a banquet. "Come, now, Rabbi. No one is watching. When will you lighten up and enjoy a piece of ham, just once in your life?"

The rabbi smiled. "At your wedding."

• • • •

A mother overheard her son saying his prayers before going to sleep: ". . .And please make Chicago the capital of Arizona."

She didn't want to intrude, but she had to find out the reason behind such a strange petition. "Why are you praying for Chicago to be the capital of Arizona?" she asked softly.

"Because that's what I answered on my geography test."

• • • •

"Come on up and join the Army of the Lord!" invited the preacher at the close of a Methodist revival service.

"Already joined," piped an impatient voice from the congregation.

"Oh? Where did you join?" asked the preacher.

"First Baptist Church, two years ago."

The preacher shook his head. "Mercy! You're not in the Army—you've joined the Navy!"

• • • •

The old preacher's sermon had been tryingly long, and he knew it. It occurred to him during the closing hymn that he might endear himself to the congregation by shortening it.

"Last verse!" he shouted as they concluded a stanza.

The organist glared at him, as did everyone else. They'd just sung the last verse.

# TRAVEL

An American couple visiting Ireland watched a truck pass by loaded with turf.

"What a great idea!" the wife exclaimed. "That's what we should do with our grass—send it out to be trimmed."

• • • •

Some cities enjoy lesser reputations than others as "destinations." Isaac Asimov used to describe Philadelphia, where he once lived, as one such metropolis. He told of the TV quiz show that offered a week-long, all-expenses-paid trip to Philly as first prize in one of its rounds. Second prize? A two-week-long, all-expenses-paid trip to Philly.

• • • •

A man vacationing in Italy happened to be in the bathroom of his hotel suite when a devastating earthquake shook the building to its frame. Pictures dropped from the walls. Plaster fell from the ceilings. Screams from adjoining rooms and sirens from the streets below filled the air.

Members of the hotel staff hurried from room to room to check on their guests. When they arrived at the American's suite, they found him cowering by the toilet. "I swear," he cried, holding up his hands and shaking his head in disbelief, "all I did was pull the chain!"

• • • •

"We just returned from vacation in Switzerland."

"Berne?"

"No, froze."

A woman stepped up to a travel desk and asked for a round-trip ticket.

"Where to?" asked the agent.

The woman looked offended. "Right back here. Where do you think?"

• • • •

Midge: "How did you like Venice?"
Esther: "It was dreadful. The streets were flooded the entire time we were there."

• • • •

A man checked into a downtown hotel. Taking the elevator to his floor, the 12th, he immediately set about locating the fire escape. He tried several doors that were locked, then found one open—but it was the women's sauna.

"Pardon me!" he cried. "I was just looking for the fire escape."

He quickly shut the door and proceeded down the hall. In a moment, he heard someone approaching from behind. He turned and saw four women, dripping wet and bound in towels and terri cloaks. "Where's the fire?" one blurted out.

• • • •

A cruise ship struck an iceberg and sank suddenly. The ship's magician found himself on a lifeboat with, among others, the crusty Scottish captain.

Four days passed. Rations were low. At length the captain turned to the magician. "Okay, lad. We give up. What ha' yah done wi' mah ship?"

A tourist in the Middle East was having a hard time shaking off a street hawker who wanted to sell him the "genuine skull of Genghis Khan."

"You're asking far too much, and I don't have luggage space to carry it home. Besides, it's repulsive—and I don't believe it's authentic."

The street seller reached into his bag and came up with a smaller skull, equally gross. He smiled broadly. "Half price—but eenfeeneetlee more valuable: skull of the great Khan, age 12."

• • • •

A con artist was trying to finesse a free train ride. When the conductor came down the aisle, the man pointed to his dog with a gesture of helpless agitation. "He ate my ticket!"

The conductor frowned. "Then I strongly suggest you buy him dessert."

• • • •

A couple vacationing in the Caribbean were irritated at the expected gratuities everywhere they turned. It seemed they couldn't enter a shop without some staff member opening the door, holding up a palm and coughing meaningfully.

But their disaffection with the island changed. One afternoon as they swam in the surf, the husband was caught in an undertow and pulled out to sea. Cramps set in; he floundered and screamed. A lifeguard down the beach heard the cries, plunged in, took the man chin-in-elbow, hauled him to the beach and successfully pumped his lungs clear.

The wife rushed to their villa and returned with her purse. "What's the going rate for this kind of thing?"

Ruth: "I heard your husband isn't taking you on vacation to Cancun this summer after all. Is it true?"

Emily: "No. It's Paris he's not taking me to this summer. Cancun is where we didn't go last summer."

• • • •

A young American professional was spending his vacation hiking alone in the African jungle when he encountered a native.

"Hello," called the American nervously.

"Nyoi, nyoi, REER-REER, nyoi, REER, nyoi," said the native, holding up his hand.

"Do you speak English?"

"Nyoi, nyoi, REER-REER, nyoi, REER, nyoi. Yes."

The American was surprised, but pleased and a bit relieved. "I'm Ben. Do you have a name?"

"Nyoi, nyoi, REER-REER, nyoi, REER, nyoi. Walter."

"Pleased to meet you, Walter. And where, might I ask, did you learn to speak English?"

"Nyoi, nyoi, REER-REER, nyoi, REER, nyoi. Short-wave radio."

• • • •

An airline pilot's voice announced in flight on the intercom, "Friends, no need to be alarmed, but we seem to be a little lost. Don't worry—we'll still arrive in plenty of time."

"Arrive where?" one passenger asked, turning to another.

# WISECRACKS

There are three kinds of people in the world:
those who can count and those who can't.

• • • •

Too many Christians want to serve the Lord
in advisory roles.

• • • •

Silence can be an excellent substitute for brilliance.

• • • •

Were it not for the last minute, few things
would be done on time.

• • • •

There's a good reason some people can't seem to mind their
own business. Usually, it's because they have either 1) no
mind or 2) no business.

• • • •

There's never a shortage of "room at the top." Replace-
ments always are needed for the ones who got up there,
then went to sleep and rolled off.

• • • •

Opportunity knocks once.
Temptation never stops knocking.

The simplest and best decisions are those which did not have to find their way through committees or channels. Consider, for example, the Ten Commandments.

• • • •

The only problem with starting a cottage industry out of your home is there's no one below you on whom to blame the mistakes.

• • • •

Some people have trouble believing anything
unless they overhear it.

• • • •

You never get something for nothing, although it may take
awhile for the billing statement to arrive.

• • • •

My hometown is so small, the only traffic light
is in the graveyard.

• • • •

Why is it that some of the most educated college gradu-
ates entering the work force seem to lack the intelligence
to match their degrees?

• • • •

According to our "National Anthem," this is a free country. Has anyone ever explained that to the IRS?

One good way to save face is to keep
the lower part of it shut.

• • • •

It was Will Rogers who pointed out that getting yourself
on the right track in life is only half the task. You'll get
run over anyway if you stand still.

• • • •

Have you seen the little 50-page bestseller called *Money
Isn't Everything?* It costs $29.95.

• • • •

If you know all the answers, then you probably
misunderstood some of the questions.

• • • •

We spend two years teaching our children to talk—and
the next 10 or 12 trying to get them to hush.

• • • •

It's good to be open-minded.
Just make sure your brains don't fall out.

• • • •

I came from a town that was so small you could chat a
spell on the phone even if you got a wrong number.

Learn to enjoy funerals. Everyone whose funeral you attend is one less person who'll be attending yours.

. . . .

Always tell the truth. That way, you don't have to remember what you've said.

. . . .

If the poor had had any money, would Robin Hood have robbed only the rich?

. . . .

Careful steering is more effective than loud horn-blowing.

. . . .

If you try sliding down the banister to success, you may get a splinter in your career.

. . . .

Children are expensive, but they last a pretty long time.

. . . .

It's easy for anyone to meet expenses. You find them everywhere.

. . . .

Government programs don't seem to have put much of a dent in poverty, but they've certainly hampered wealth.

It's better to ask stupid questions
than make stupid mistakes.

• • • •

Smoking, commented Fletcher Knebel,
is one of the leading causes of statistics.

• • • •

There never seems to be enough time to do things right—
but there's always enough time to do them
right the second time.

• • • •

A day without sunshine is like a night without moonlight.

• • • •

Time may pass quickly or slowly, depending
on how far you are from the nearest rest room.

• • • •

The best way to become a popular member of a
committee is to be the first one to move for adjournment.
Everyone else wants to, but they don't want to
appear lazy.

• • • •

Do something brilliant and no one is watching.
Do something stupid and the whole world is watching.

Did you ever wonder how, according to advertised statistics, two out of three American doctors can recommend one pain reliever while three out of four doctors recommend a rival and four out of five doctors simultaneously recommend yet a third brand?

• • • •

We recognize most opportunities after they've knocked on the doors of our business competitors.

• • • •

I'm a man of many good intentions—but
I'm not fast enough to keep up with them.

• • • •

Don't invest your money in anything
that requires regular feeding.

• • • •

Living in a small town makes it easy to resist temptation.

• • • •

The cost of living doesn't seem to affect its popularity.

• • • •

And sliced bread is the greatest thing since. . . what?

# THE WORKPLACE

"I remember when we had 12-hour workdays, then 10, then 8 and now 7," said a veteran on the job. "You know, it's no easier getting up at 8 o'clock than it was getting up at 5 o'clock."

An administrator was interviewing a job applicant. "And where did you rank among your class at high school graduation?" she asked.

"Fifty-fifth."

"Out of how many students?"

"Fifty-five."

"My, my. I suppose it would be difficult to come up with a worse record than that."

"Oh, by no means."

"How do you figure?"

"Well, for example, I know people who graduated in classes of 500 or more."

• • • •

A rail official was interviewing an applicant for traffic controller. "Now, Len," he said, "what would you do first if you noticed on the light board up here that an eastbound train was on the same track as a westbound train and, if not alerted, they would collide about. . .here, at Silverton?"

Len responded immediately, "I'd get on the phone and notify my brother Walter over near Silverton."

The official was puzzled. "Why? Does your brother work for the railroad?"

"No, sir—but he ain't never seen a good train wreck before."

Petty theft had been a growing problem at the office, and the secretary confided to the boss that she was looking for a place to hide her pocketbook while she was on the job.

"Try the filing cabinet," the boss said. "We never find anything in there."

• • • •

A chemical engineer lost his job as a result of downsizing and ended up resorting to a career service. After three months, the best report his agent had to offer was, "Nothing yet—but don't worry. We have your resumé in the hands of corporate personnel administrators across the US and in nine foreign countries."

"What you're telling me," the engineer said, "is that I'm now unemployed in 10 different countries."

• • • •

"Do you believe in ghosts?"

The worker thought it odd to be asked that question by his boss. He scratched his head and said, "Well, I suppose I do. . .maybe."

"I guess I do, too. Late yesterday, after you'd left to go to your uncle's funeral, he came in looking for you."

• • • •

A worker complained to her boss, "My pay is $10 short this week."

"Oh, that's because the bookkeeper realized she'd been paying you $5 too much for the past two weeks. Frankly, I'm surprised you didn't report it then."

"No fair!" the worker howled. "One mistake I can over-look. Even two. But three—I won't stand for it."

"Who should we notify in case of an accident?" the administrator asked a new employee while filling out the paperwork.

The employee thought a moment. "The first person you can flag down."

• • • •

"Age" the employment application prompted.

"Nuclear," the elderly man wrote.

• • • •

One worker to another: "I've used up all my sick days, so tomorrow I reckon I'll just have to call in dead."

• • • •

A farmer visiting Cincinnati gazed up at a sign proclaiming "JONES MANUFACTURING, INC."

"My," he said, rubbing his chin. "So that's where all the Joneses come from."

• • • •

The firm's administrator really was taken by the character of the job applicant, but she strongly suspected the woman was past retirement age.

"On your application," the administrator remarked tactfully, "I see your birthday is the same as my mother's: September the 6th. May I ask what year?"

"Every year," came the stoic reply.

A teen-age boy had searched for a job long and hard and was devastated to be turned down for a position working the counter at a fast-food restaurant. The reason, explained the manager, was the boy's illiteracy.

Undaunted, he began doing people's yard work, then learned the basics of routine landscaping and ultimately acquired a local reputation as a knowledgeable, professional landscaper. He opened his own shrub nursery, which led to a chain of nurseries. By age 35 he was the town's wealthiest citizen—and remained illiterate.

"Just imagine where you might be," his wife mused one day, "if you could read and write."

• • • •

Two prominent businessmen were asked to share their secrets of success.

"I lie awake at night thinking up ideas," said one.

"I stay awake days," said the other.

• • • •

"Did you hear Jim just got canned?" one employee asked another.

"What for?"

"For good."

• • • •

A carpenter fell two stories and landed with a thud on his back.

"What happened?" asked a coworker, rushing to his side.

"I'm not sure," the victim said. "I just got here."

Two workers on coffee break were gazing out the window at huge white snowflakes wafting to the ground. "I love snew," commented one.

"What's snew?"

"Oh, not much. What's new with you?"

• • • •

A plant manager was out on the floor one day when he saw a man leaning against a utility shelf, sipping a soda. It wasn't even close to break time, and the manager was furious.

"What do you get paid, sir?" he asked the lounger.

"About $20 an hour."

"Outrageous!" fumed the manager. "Come with me."

He led the man to his office, calculated a week's pay at $20 an hour, paged the company paymaster to write a check immediately, paid the man off and told him, "Now get out. You're fired. There's nothing I hate worse than a loafer."

The man pocketed the check and walked out without a word.

"By the way, who's your immediate supervisor?" the manager called after him.

The loafer turned and replied, "Mr. Black over at XYZ Parcel Service is my boss. He sent me here to make a pick-up, and I've been waiting about 20 minutes for your people to get it ready."

• • • •

Apprentice: "How do you know whether to use a nail or a screw?"

Carpenter: "Try the nail. If it splits the board, you should have used the screw."

It was 11 a.m. when Mickie finally arrived at work—limping, her head half smothered in a thick, white bandage, her left arm in a sling. Her supervisor frowningly watched her punch the time clock.

"And what's all this?" the boss demanded. "You're two hours late."

"I'm really sorry," Mickie said. "Someone tripped me at the top of the subway stairs and I tumbled all the way to the bottom of the first flight. When I tried to get up, I didn't realize I'd sprained an ankle, and I fell down the second flight—and then some man trying to help me lost his own balance, and we both plunged to the bottom of the third flight."

Still frowning, the supervisor calculated, "You say three flights of steps took you two hours. . . ?"

• • • •

Members of a corporate management team were sharply divided in assessing a department head candidate. Panned one, "I think he's far too caustic for this position."

"Who cares what he costs?" rejoined another. "He's knows how to run the department better than we do."

------

We want to hear from you! If you've got a great joke you'd like to submit for inclusion in *Great Clean Jokes for Grown-Up Kids #2*, please mail to: Jokes, PO Box 719, Uhrichsville, OH 44683.

**Great Clean Jokes for Kids** by Dan Harmon. You'll get a giggle a minute with *Great Clean Jokes for Kids*—page after page of the funniest jokes and easiest-to-remember punchlines ever written for kids, ages 6 to 10.

**$1.99**

**Fun Facts About the Bible You Never Knew** by Robyn Martins. Games, word searches, quizzes, fill-in-the-blanks—all in this one glorious edition. Youth group meetings, Sunday school classes, and Bible studies will never be the same again!

**$2.49**

Available wherever books are sold.

**Or order from:**

Barbour Publishing, Inc.

P.O. Box 719

Uhrichsville, Ohio 44683

http://www.barbourbooks.com

If you order by mail, add $2.00 to your order for shipping.

Prices subject to change without notice.